The Soothsayer's Handbook-A Guide to Bad Signs & Good Vibrations by Elinor Lander Horwitz

J. B. LIPPINCOTT COMPANY/Philadelphia and New York

U.S. Library of Congress Cataloging in Publication Data

Horwitz, Elinor Lander.
  The soothsayer's handbook.

  SUMMARY: A do-it-yourself guide to reading character and telling fortunes
using ESP, astrology, palmistry, numerology, playing cards, tea leaves, dice,
dominoes, and crystal balls.

  1. Divination—Juvenile literature. 2. Extrasensory perception—Juvenile
literature. [1. Divination. 2. Extrasensory perception]. I. Title.
BF1751.H67   133.3   76–172143
ISBN–0–397–31538–4

for
TONY

Contents

there was a lack of demand for the services of men or women gifted in predicting what was to come.

The use of animals as omens began before the dawn of history. Men sacrificed an animal to the gods and then examined its liver and intestines to determine by their shape and form what the deity willed. Another ancient method of divination involved observing the flights of birds, and holy men were also expected to understand the language of the birds. In the Cameroons today certain large spiders, considered sacred, are used in fortune-telling. Special magic cards, made from leaves, are put in the spider's pen, and the way in which the insect moves the cards as he walks back and forth over them provides the pattern in which the fates of men can be read. All over the world there are people who find bad-news-to-come in the hooting of an owl or the birth of a three-legged calf.

Cards, dice, and coins are used as means of divination across the globe. Throwing coins is an essential part of the ancient Chinese method of determining rules of fate and human conduct according to the ancient "Book of Changes" or *I Ching*. Readable signs are also seen in the shapes of embers after a fire, the tea leaves left in a cup, the images in a thin spread of sand or in a crystal ball. Telling the future by signs also takes the form of bibliomancy, the practice of opening the Bible at random and pointing to a verse—and then reading and interpreting it as warning of the consequences of an intended act or as the answer to a question.

Belief in "lucky" and "unlucky" numbers has guided the course of action of countless people throughout all time. Predicting the future by interpreting numerical coincidences is a basic technique in divination—as well as in gambling. Many contemporary prophets foretold John F. Kennedy's death on the grounds that every American president elected at twenty-year intervals since

1840 has died in office: Harrison (elected 1840), Lincoln (elected 1860), Garfield (elected 1880), McKinley (elected 1900), Harding (elected 1920), Roosevelt (elected 1940). Kennedy was elected in 1960.

Graphology—the practice of reading character by examining handwriting—is not included in this book because, unlike the other methods mentioned, it has some scientific accreditation. Penmanship is a conscious act over which man has considerable control and many psychologists consider it a form of personality expression.

An aspect of divination that does not depend on reading signs is prophecy, in which a person considered specially inspired is able to foresee, prophesize, predict—by divine revelation— without the assistance of *any* hints from actual objects. The inter-pretation of dreams, an age-old prophetic gift familiar to every-one from the biblical story of Joseph, is based on the belief that the invisible images which make up our dreams are symbols of future events in the physical world. Although we are not dealing with prophets, seers, saints, mediums, witches, or warlocks in this book, there is no question about the fact that the best future-tell-ers, fortune-tellers, and character-readers invariably have a touch of the seer in them. Do you? To enable you to find out, we have devoted the first chapter to the vital subject of testing your sixth sense, or extrasensory perception.

Although diviners still warn of great floods, wars, and other disasters, most of us today rely on such authorities as scientists and news analysts when we try to see into the ever-mysterious future of our country, our planets, and the universe. But when it comes to our own personal fate, few of us can resist learning what is written in our stars and in our hands, or in the spread of the cards . . . or in the tea leaves . . . or in the magical date of our birth—whether we believe a word of it or not.

skill decreases with fatigue, just like the ability to do difficult math problems or reading comprehension tests. Another observation was that people who believe in the existence of extrasensory perception—whom he called "sheep"—scored notably higher than the disbelievers, whom he named "goats."

Are you a sheep or a goat?

Before we come to the testing, here are some further facts about the three divisions of ESP.

CLAIRVOYANCE

At Dr. Rhine's laboratory, methods were devised to test for clairvoyance, but many of the people who volunteered to be tested were already certain that they possessed this ability because of strange clairvoyant experiences in their everyday lives. Many people of all ages have been startled by sudden inner knowledge about something which, on investigation, turned out to be true.

One story repeated in many books on clairvoyance concerns a ten-year-old girl in a small town who was walking to school reading her math book. She suddenly had a vision of her mother lying as if dead on the floor of a bedroom at home with a lace handkerchief at her side. Although the child had left home less than fifteen minutes earlier and her mother had seemed well, she was so certain of her vision that she rushed to the doctor's house, reported that her mother was gravely ill, and then hurried with the doctor to her home. They found the woman lying just as her daughter had pictured her, and the lace handkerchief was on the floor nearby. The mother had had a heart attack and the doctor saved her life.

Well, most people have not had such dramatic experiences as this, but many have been at times seized with an idea, a "hunch," that something was wrong with a beloved relative. Many people, acting on this notion, have rushed to the telephone —and sometimes they're right, although often they're wrong. There's a difference between a clairvoyant and a plain old worrier.

It's interesting that psychic experiences almost always seem to deal with disaster. You never read of a child whose vision revealed her mother leaping about the house with joy because she had just won the Irish Sweepstakes. (Many gamblers, however, are able to summon visions of *themselves* in this situation. Usually, they're wrong. Anyhow, if they were right we'd call it precognition rather than clairvoyance, and that comes later.)

Typical reports of clairvoyant experiences are: A mother felt a sharp pain on the day her soldier son was shot on another continent; a daughter wakened in the night filled with foreboding and found in the morning that her father had had a fatal auto accident at that hour; a girl was overwhelmed at her desk with feelings of fear and nausea and ran to the amusement park to find her twin sister screaming in terror at the top of the stalled Ferris wheel. Sometimes the stories are less grim. A clairvoyant looking for a lost ring suddenly has a vision of it lying in an ice cube tray in the refrigerator; hunters "sense" that the prey is near although they neither see, hear, nor smell it; dogs somehow know their way home after jumping from a car ten miles away, although they've never been off the block.

The feeling of having been somewhere before, when you know you haven't, or of having had a particular conversation with someone earlier, is so common that its name, *déjà vu* (French for "already seen"), has become a medical term. Many people walking in a foreign city for the first time have turned a corner and then been seized with strong and eerie déjà vu sensations. To others it has happened entering a strange house or restaurant.

ments with his gifted wife. Mrs. Sinclair would sit quietly in her room while Mr. Sinclair, in another room, drew a simple object: a spoon, a star, a cat's head, an umbrella, etc. Mrs. Sinclair was able in a large number of cases to receive the image and draw, in response, a very similar picture. She also reproduced drawings made by a relative in another state and by a secretary, who delivered her sketches in opaque envelopes which Mrs. Sinclair held while receiving the image. Here are some of the drawings made by Mr. Sinclair and reproduced telepathically by Mrs. Sinclair who was seated in another room. Mr. Sinclair drew the

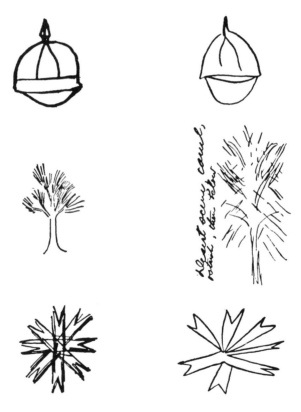

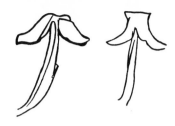

pictures on the left and Mrs. Sinclair's attempts to match them are shown on the right.

You can easily try a test of this sort with a member of your family or a friend. You might simply sit back to back with pads in your laps. One person draws a picture, concentrates very hard on what he has drawn, and calls out, "Ready!" Then the other person tries to draw the same object. See how you can do.

PRECOGNITION

If the schoolgirl we spoke of earlier, who saw a vision of her mother on the floor, had instead sensed that her mother was calling to her and had seen her conscious but helpless with a broken leg, her experience would have been one of telepathy rather than clairvoyance. If the child had awakened during the night with a vision of her mother falling ill in the morning, we would call it precognition.

The Bible is filled with stories of prophetic dreams which foretell the future and of encounters with mystical people. The Witch of Endor was consulted because of her precognitive skills much as the Greeks sought advice of the Oracle at Delphi.

Shakespeare frequently heightened the dramatic effect of his plays by using witches and soothsayers. The witches in Macbeth hail him as a future king and later call out that he cannot be harmed by any man born of woman or until Birnam Wood, near his castle, moves against him. A soothsayer tells Julius Caesar to beware the Ides of March. His wife, Calpurnia, has frightening dreams the night before the Ides and pleads with him not to go to the senate on that day. His royal seers also tell him to stay at home because in slaughtering an animal they have found that it has no heart, a very dreadful sign indeed. Caesar goes, and is assassinated on the steps of the senate.

Many contemporary seers claim to have foreseen President Kennedy's assassination. Other stories abound. The boxer Marcel Cerdan was warned by a fortune-teller, whom he consulted about the results of a coming match, that he would be killed in a plane crash on his way to the city where the fight was to take place. He ignored the warning and died when his plane went down in the ocean.

As is the case with other forms of ESP, stories about precognition usually concern people who "see" dreadful scenes of themselves or loved ones dead, crashing in automobiles, being burned in fires, suffering grave illnesses and bloody wounds. Joan of Arc dreamed precognitively that she'd be wounded in battle at Orléans. She also displayed clairvoyance by knowing the real king, Charles VII, who had deceptively placed someone else on the throne while he stood disguised among a group of courtiers. It's easy to see that visions, voices, and the gift of prophecy can be dangerous gifts. We all know what happened to St. Joan.

TESTING YOUR ESP

Are you ready to test your ESP? Do you frequently have correct hunches that you're going to get a certain grade on an exam, and then you do? Do you and your best friend often think of the same thing at the same time? Do you dream something is going to happen and then it does? Do you often guess correctly in guessing games? Furthermore, does your mother, father, sister, or brother have such abilities? Grandmother? Uncle? Great-aunt? Experiments at Duke University have shown that ESP may be hereditary. Many people tested came to the clinic because they felt there was a history of clairvoyant or telepathic ability in the family. Often it was described as "intuition." Do you have intuitions about people? Does your mother? Are you a twin? Twins are very likely to find they can communicate with each other telepathically. Do you feel your new friend is on your "wave length"? Perhaps he really is. Test *him* too. Do you consider yourself lucky? Do others consider you lucky?

Most ESP testing is done with cards, including those methods devised at Dr. Rhine's Duke University laboratory, which are designed to be repeated over and over. Obviously, you can't retake our picture test to see how you would do a second time, because once you take it, you will know the answers. That's why it must only be considered a preliminary to discovering whether you do indeed have a sixth sense. The laws of chance alone may help you to guess right in many instances, whether you are psychic or not. The element of chance can be ruled out only in a long series of repeated tests.

PICTURE TEST

There are no hidden clues in this test that will help you determine the right answers. The only way you can answer correctly is by concentrating on the pictures until you feel you have found the answer by using your extrasensory perception. This test does not give you a fifty-fifty chance of guessing correctly since some questions involve three possibilities to choose from and some have even more. Therefore, if you score as many as three correctly, you may have ESP. If you score over five right, you're great. Answers appear on page 155.

1. Tony and his friend Tony are thinking of a number between one and five. They are concentrating very hard on the number and the photographer is saying it aloud. Do you know what it is?

2. Frasie is holding two ginger ale cans. One is full and one is empty. Which is the full can?

3. David, Larry, and Tony are going out to play baseball. Which of them is holding the ball?

4. Larry and Jane are playing cards. One of them needs the seven of hearts and the other one is holding it. Which player is looking at the seven of hearts?

5. The twins are sitting on the stairs being very serious so you can look carefully and tell which of them is Anne and which is Alice.

6. Brian, Tony, and Josh are all good athletes. Which of them rides the unicycle?

7 & 8. In picture 7 are two sisters and their brother. Picture 8 shows two brothers and their sister. One child in each family was born in March. Can you spot them?

9. Angela and Tony are showing each other their kittens. Which one is the female?

10. Jane and Tony are looking at a single bright color. They are concentrating on the color and thinking of its name. Can you tell which color it is?

11. Look at the seven girls and boys in this picture very carefully. They know the answers to the three following questions. Do you?

  a. Which one can play the violin?
  b. Which one can juggle?
  c. Which one has ridden a bucking bronco?

12. Brian wants Angela to guess which hand has the penny. Can you tell?

COIN TOSSING TEST

If you toss a penny and guess how it has fallen your chances of guessing correctly are fifty-fifty since there are only two alternatives. However, if you only toss it 5 times you might very well happen to make 4 lucky guesses. If you toss it 500 times, however, your correct guesses will probably be pretty close to 250. If on 500 tosses you guess right 400 times, something's up: either you're psychic or you're cheating.

The coin toss can be used as an ESP test in each of three categories as described earlier in the chapter. Try to get a feeling of how the coin has landed or will land rather than simply guessing. Test yourself with a coin for clairvoyance, telepathy, and precognition, flipping at least twenty-five times in each category. Keep careful count of your "hits"—the word ESP testers use for correct answers. Are you better at telepathy or clairvoyance? Do you show a score of over 50 percent correct in any of these areas? In all three? Fabulous.

CARD TESTS

Now let's get on to the card tests. First we will use a regular pack of playing cards. You will need to make up a score sheet. Copy the following score sheet. The figures across the top refer to the number of series you do—the number of times you go through the entire deck of cards.

NAME _____ DATE _____

TESTER _____

	1		2		3		4		5	
	CALL	CARD	CALL	CARD	CALL	CARD	CALL	CARD	CALL	CARD
1										
2										
3										
4										
5										
6										
7										
8										
9										
10										
11										
12										
13										
14										
15										
16										
17										
18										
19										
20										
21										
22										
23										
24										
25										
↓ 52										

TOTAL

1. Sit down at a table with a friend and put a deck of cards between you, face down. Have your friend take the score sheet and enter your calls. Call one card at a time. Place your hand on the top card, remove it, and place it, still face down, to the right of the deck. Then call it and your friend will write the call in the correct space. On this try call color only, red or black. Go through the entire deck without looking at the face of any card. When you're finished, turn over the deck and have your friend write down in the card column what each card actually was. The top card, when you turn over the deck, will be the first card you called. Then check for correct matching and write your total number of hits at the bottom of the column. Here is part of a sample score card for a test of this sort.

	CALL	CARD
1	R	B
2	B	B
3	R	R
4	B	R
5	B	B

To turn this test into a telepathy test, take the score card and sit across the room. Have your friend lift each card separately and look at it. Then you make your call, which you will write down, trying with great concentration to read his mind correctly. Any score above 25 hits is excellent.

2. Using the same procedure, reduce your chances to one in four instead of one out of two by guessing suit, rather than color, this time. This is much more difficult, and if you score more than 13 correct out of fifty-two cards in this test you are definitely exceeding the law of averages and may feel you have shown evidence of ESP ability.

		1		2	
	CALL	CARD	CALL	CARD	
1	Clubs	clubs	hearts	diamonds	
2	diamonds	spades	diamonds	clubs	
3	diamonds	hearts	diamonds	hearts	
4	spades	hearts	diamonds	diamonds	
5	hearts	diamonds	spades	spades	
6	hearts	hearts	clubs	hearts	

3. To make the test a great deal *more* difficult, try guessing the card by its number or picture. This test gives you fourteen alternatives, or one chance in fourteen of making a correct guess. A score in this test of 3–4 correct out of 52 is average. Anything above that is excellent.

Now we will go on to tests using special ESP cards. At Duke University a set of twenty-five cards was devised. Five simple symbols were used and there were five cards with each of these symbols. One card had a square, one a circle, one a star, one a cross, and one a wavy line. Using these cards you have a one-in-five chance of success, or five hits as average on each runthrough of the twenty-five cards. You can make your own set of cards using the symbols chosen by Dr. Rhine or any symbols—or colors —you wish, as long as they aren't easily confused with each other. Regular index cards are fine for this purpose. Use a felt watercolor pen or a crayon to draw the symbol on the unlined side of the card. You can use the same score sheet that you used for the playing card tests, numbered to 25 instead of 52.

If in a twenty-five-card ESP test you consistently average more than five hits per series you would be considered to show strong evidence of ESP. Dr. Rhine's best subjects consistently scored several points above five, often about seven or eight. On a few

 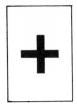   

occasions a subject called twenty-five correct cards in a row! One
of these times the subject was a nine-year-old child who had
been promised a fifty-cent reward if she achieved a perfect score.
On another occasion it was a divinity student who had consistently scored above average but who had become bored with the
test. To stimulate him to higher effort he too was challenged
with each card and rewarded for correct answers. In five runs
you can expect to score 25 hits by pure chance. A score of 33–34
is considered very encouraging, and 67 and up, excellent. The
odds against obtaining an "encouraging" score by pure chance
are between 10–1 and 20–1. If scores are in the range we've
called "excellent" the odds are 100–1 or higher.

Here is part of a score sheet for a test using ESP cards and a
table of laws of chance in the tests we've described.

	1		2	
	CALL	CARD	CALL	CARD
1	□	+	～	～
2	○	★	+	+
3	+	+	○	□
4	○	○	★	+

Probability	
coin flipping	$\frac{1}{2}$
cards-color	$\frac{1}{2}$
cards-suit	$\frac{1}{4}$
ESP cards	$\frac{1}{5}$
cards-number or picture	$\frac{1}{14}$

Other alternatives for ESP tests are calling numerals from one to ten, which can be written on cards, or calling letters of the alphabet. The averages in these instances would, of course, be $\frac{1}{10}$ or $\frac{1}{26}$.

In carrying out ESP tests it is of the greatest importance that no hints of any sort be given to the person being tested. Make sure that cards, as they are used over and over, do not develop distinctive markings: a slight tear, a bent corner, etc. If you are the sender in a telepathy test, do not reveal by gesture or expression anything about the card, or indicate whether the receiver is giving correct or incorrect answers.

If you have discovered that you do indeed have ESP you are destined for great success as a fortune-teller. You will know much about your subject's personality, circumstances, and destiny that less gifted people will miss. If, like most of us, you do not have ESP, do not despair. Read on and learn the rules for understanding character and telling fortunes by interpretation of signs—and use your imagination.

2
Astrology

Man made maps of the heavens long before he attempted to map the earth. The reason is probably obvious. Until more advanced civilizations polluted the air, ancient people looked up and saw, in all directions, a luminous sky filled with brilliant heavenly bodies. By careful observation they could note that these bodies moved in fixed groups, which we now call constellations. It became evident that the sun, which appeared by day, and the moon, which appeared by night, affected such natural happenings as the tides, the growth of crops, the regular rotation of the seasons. It must have seemed perfectly logical that these astral marvels—thought of as great and powerful gods—also controlled the fate of nations and events in the lives of men. The earth, known only as the patch of land on which one had been born, must have seemed a pretty insignificant bit of territory compared to the magnificence of the great dome of the sky.

The ancient Chaldean and Babylonian astrologers, who lived in areas of present-day Iraq, spoke only of predicting the welfare of the country and the ruler, who personified the state. It was not until the sixth century B.C., in the Golden Age of Greece, that as-

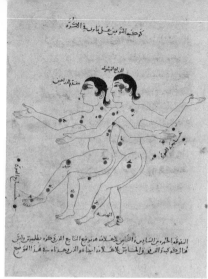

These four plates are reproduced from one of the oldest surviving Islamic books. It is titled *The Book of Fixed Stars* and was written by the famous Arab astronomer Abd al-Rahman. The book bears the date A.D. 1009/10. These four plates show Gemini, Virgo, Sagittarius, and Aquarius.

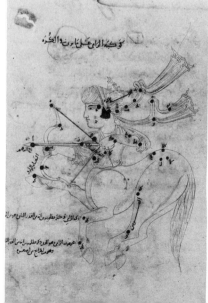

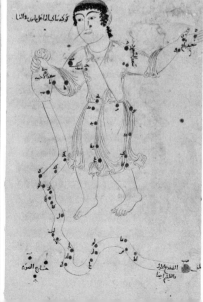

trology was seen as pertaining to the lives of ordinary mortals and a horoscope became available to anyone willing to pay. Astrology remained popular throughout the Middle Ages in both Europe and Asia. As time went on, the branch of astrology that studied the movements of heavenly bodies became the basis for the new science of astronomy, but the other branch, which concerned itself with predicting plagues, wars, earthquakes, and the characters and destinies of individuals, survived. Today, it is estimated that in the United States alone over five thousand astrologers are at work drawing up individual horoscopes, and virtually every major newspaper and a great many periodicals here and in Great Britain and other European countries have astrological columns. Computers have been programmed to take basic facts of time and place of birth, perform astrological calculations, and punch out lengthy reports of the subject's character, abilities, favorable vocational possibilities, relationships to others, health, wealth, etc. In India horoscopes are drawn for each infant at the time of birth, and in many Near Eastern and Asian countries astrologers are always consulted before wedding dates are set, business decisions made, or affairs of state determined. Over the centuries astrology has been prevalent in virtually every part of the globe.

THE ZODIAC

The zodiac is an imaginary division of the heavens into twelve zones, each one named for the constellation which occupies its area. The constellations, in turn, are named for the "pictures" that ancient people saw in their star patterns. The sun can be found in each zone for approximately thirty days of the year, and therefore the twelve divisions of the zodiac correspond roughly to the twelve months of the year. The astrological calendar, how-

Signs of the Zodiac	*Symbols*	*Dates*
ARIES The Ram	♈	March 22–April 20
TAURUS The Bull	♉	April 21–May 20
GEMINI The Twins	♊	May 21–June 21
CANCER The Crab	♋	June 22–July 23
LEO The Lion	♌	July 24–August 23
VIRGO The Virgin	♍	August 24–September 23
LIBRA The Scales	♎	September 24–October 23
SCORPIO The Scorpion	♏	October 24–November 22
SAGITTARIUS The Archer	♐	November 23–December 21
CAPRICORN The Goat	♑	December 22–January 20
AQUARIUS The Water-Bearer	♒	January 21–February 19
PISCES The Fish	♓	February 20–March 21

ever, begins on March 22, when the sun enters the sign of Aries, and ends when it leaves the twelfth sign, Pisces, on March 21. If you consult a number of astrology books you will find that the dates of the astrological months vary slightly. One, for example, will list Aquarius as January 20–February 18 and another as January 21–February 19. This is because the precise date on which the sun enters and leaves a particular zone varies according to which part of the world you're in, as the sun moves from east to west. If your birthday is, for instance, January 20, an astrologer can consult charts which tell the exact position of the heavenly bodies at various times of the day of your birth, and if you can tell him where you were born and at what exact time he can tell you whether you are really a Capricornian or an Aquarian.

The charts used for such calculations are also necessary for making up a complete horoscope. A horoscope is simply a chart of the heavens as seen from a particular place at a particular time, and it includes not only the position of the sun but also the position of the moon and of the planets, which move on courses of varying distance. Astrologers believe that you are endowed at the moment of birth with certain characteristics determined by the heavens, and that the influence of all these bodies—the sun, the moon, and the planets—begin to shape your development from the moment of your first breath.

If you would like to see some of the complex charts used in drawing individual horoscopes, you might look at a book called an Ephemeris, available in bookshops and libraries, which gives the exact positions of the moon and planets on each day of the year for many many years back. The astrologers must translate these readings, which are in Greenwich mean time (five hours later than eastern standard time) into the correct time zone for the latitude and longitude of your birthplace. Here is a horoscope for Napoleon Bonaparte, born 9:51 A.M. on August 15, 1769, in Corsica.

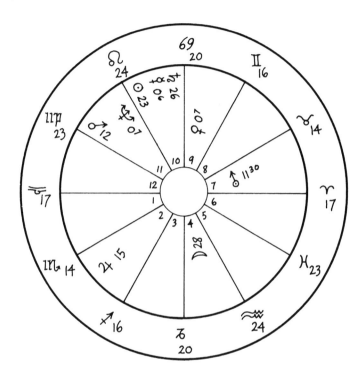

The numbers written near the symbols indicate the exact position, in degrees, of the heavenly bodies and their relationship to the pielike divisions of space in the zodiac. The zodiac symbols are shown on page 39. Here are the symbols for the sun, moon, and planets, and the aspects of your life they are thought to influence.

SUN   honor and power

MOON   desires and emotions

MERCURY   the intellect

VENUS   love

MARS   courage, enthusiasm, and war

JUPITER   religion, science, and philosophy

SATURN   perseverance, delays, and disappointments

URANUS   inventiveness, genius, good or bad luck

NEPTUNE   mysticism, art, and poetry

We are not, in this book, going to chart or read horoscopes, because there is no space to include all the very detailed necessary charts, and the problem of *interpreting* all this information is extremely complex. Although you may some day have an astrologer cast your own complete horoscope and interpret the meanings of the positions of the moon and planets at your birth, the most im-

A set of twelve Israeli stamps reproduces the signs of the zodiac.

portant sign and the central key to character analysis is the sun sign. This chapter will teach you to know your sun signs. Astrologers say that knowing your sun sign alone gives you about 80 or 90 percent of the accurate facts about yourself. If, however, you are a Scorpio, for instance, and the description of the Scorpio personality simply isn't as much like you as you think it should be, it is possible that your ascendant—the planet which appeared at the horizon at the time of your birth—is in Gemini and has given you strong Gemini leanings. The moon's position may also have greatly altered your Scorpio tendencies.

By the way, your sign is thought by astrologers to govern your appearance as well as your personality. Here is another chart, which gives the physical descriptions of true zodiac types. See how your friends and relatives check out on this influence of the stars. Look also at the famous people listed after the description of each sun sign and see whether they conform to type and bear physical resemblance to each other.

ARIES: Medium height, spare, dark hair and skin, muscular, fast-moving, likely to have bushy eyebrows.

TAURUS: Short, thickset, dark eyes and hair, strong movements, likely to have a large mouth and a musical voice.

GEMINI: Tall, long limbs, fair complexion, slender and agile, delicate features, quick movements.

CANCER: Medium height with long arms and legs, broad-shouldered, small face with light eyes, but likely to have a pronounced jaw and large feet.

LEO: Broad in build with a large head, ruddy complexion, stately posture. Face is often described as having "character."

VIRGO: Compact, average height with wiry build, dark hair, regular features. May be very handsome.

LIBRA: Tall and shapely, brown or black hair and good complexion, inclined to be curvaceous if female, with unusually pleasant voice.

SCORPIO: Middle height, ruddy or swarthy coloring, muscular but inclined to obesity, heavy facial features.

SAGITTARIUS: Taller than average in build, unable to sit still and uses hands a good deal to gesture while talking, high forehead, long nose.

CAPRICORN: Slender with dark hair and skin. The face is often long and thin and the body is graceful and movements quick.

AQUARIUS: Inclined to be heavy and slow-moving, fair-haired, expressive face with high coloring, likely to have perpetually cold hands and feet.

PISCES: Short and rather fleshy, pale soft skin and silky thin hair. Likely to be graceful in movement with well-shaped hands and feet, and dimples are common.

This seventeenth-century astrology
book shows man's body ruled by
the zodiac. Each sign of the zodiac
controls the health of a different
part of the anatomy.

The rest of the chapter is devoted to understanding sun signs. When you read about the sun signs you will note interesting similarities, which you have probably already been aware of, between yourself and your sister, brother, father, or mother. You might like to draw up an astrological family tree with the sun sign of each person written under the name. See if the people you'd always been told were "alike" have the same or compatible signs. Here is a chart of compatible signs, which may also be particularly meaningful if you are joining with someone in friendship, in marriage, or in a business matter.

Sign	Compatible Sign
Aries	Aries, Leo, or Sagittarius
Taurus	Taurus, Virgo, or Capricorn
Gemini	Gemini, Libra, or Aquarius
Cancer	Cancer, Scorpio, or Pisces
Leo	Leo, Aries, or Sagittarius
Virgo	Virgo, Taurus, or Capricorn
Libra	Libra, Gemini, or Aquarius
Scorpio	Scorpio, Cancer, or Pisces
Sagittarius	Sagittarius, Aries, or Leo
Capricorn	Capricorn, Taurus, or Virgo
Aquarius	Aquarius, Gemini, or Libra
Pisces	Pisces, Cancer, or Scorpio

This table is based on the classification of zodiac signs into fiery signs (Aries, Sagittarius, and Leo); earthy signs (Taurus, Virgo, and Capricorn); airy signs (Aquarius, Libra, and Gemini); and watery signs (Cancer, Scorpio, and Pisces).

People born under the earthy signs are marked by personalities that are practical and steady, energetic and strong. Those born under the airy signs tend to be intellectual folk who are interested in the arts and sciences, and who express themselves well in speech and writing. The fiery signs confer on those born under their influence ambition and courage. These people are often enthusiastic leaders. Those whose birth dates fall under the watery signs are emotional and loving people, who are sympathetic, warm daydreamers—and likely to be impractical. Although many a man of action has married, with great happiness, a shy and sensitive woman, astrologers really do not believe that "opposites attract" as a general rule.

Often when you meet someone you feel at ease with immediately, you will find that your signs are the same or are in sympathy with each other. Astrology may explain why it is that Sally or Mary or David or Pete is the person who really understands you best. A study of sun signs will also help you to realize why Phyllis is so tidy about all her possessions, why Marian is fearful about entering into games and speaking in front of the class, why Mark is boastful, and Allen is always getting into fights, and Lisa is so bossy . . . and why your brother talks so much . . . and why you are always criticized for not paying attention in math class. If you're a baby-sitter, by the way, you can learn a lot about why some babies are so stubborn and others so smiley and yet others go into tantrums. And if your cat is a Leo he thinks he's a lion and he expects constant attention, praise, and respect, or he'll growl and sulk . . . or hadn't you noticed? And if your dog is an earthy Taurus, give up trying to teach him to love little Leo—they've been hopelessly incompatible from birth.

ARIES MARCH 22–APRIL 20

People born when the sun is in Aries grow up to be courageous, ambitious, and forceful. If you are an Arietian you have noticed from earliest childhood that friends depend on you for advice. You enjoy jobs which give you opportunities for personal leadership. Your vitality and energy make you an asset to organizations, committees planning new projects, and all sorts of clubs and action groups.

Aries-born men and women must avoid being overly aggressive and reckless, however. If they're not careful they may upset the harmony of their home, their office, or their school. If their energies are not guided by a dose of restraint they may rush into ventures which they are incapable of completing. The intense desire of Arietians to lead others and to be boss makes them uncooperative workers when they are not in charge.

Aries-born boys and girls can be incredibly stubborn. Although they love to give advice they will rarely listen if it is contrary to what they want to hear. They can be tactless and impatient with other people who are less bright and able than themselves, but they are almost never cruel. As young children they tend to be selfish, however, and must be taught to share toys as well as to develop a sense of responsibility about schoolwork later on.

Socially they are clever conversationalists—optimistic and witty people who enjoy a good time and who are an asset to a party. Their enthusiasm is particularly delightful and contagious. They are, however, given to overdoing their pleasures and must guard against overeating and excessive smoking and drinking as they get older. They are also accident-prone and tend to be careless about their health.

People born under the sign of the Ram do not create an atmosphere of tranquility and serenity, but rather of liveliness, brightness, enthusiasm, and boldness. They insist on freedom but are very possessive of people they love. They are rebels by nature and will defy authority all their lives, although they enjoy exert-

48

ing their power over others. Their characters are full of contradictions—and they are never dull.

Famous people born under the sign of Aries include:

Charlemagne	Doris Day
Leonardo da Vinci	Robert Frost
Charlie Chaplin	Warren Beatty
Booker T. Washington	Johann Sebastian Bach
Harry Houdini	Tennessee Williams
Arturo Toscanini	Marlon Brando

TAURUS APRIL 21–MAY 20

Taurians are steadfast, systematic, persevering, and affectionate people. They are warm and loving, but not given to romantic talk, little gifts, and such. The term "strong silent type" best describes a typical Taurian.

Taurians have the power of the Bull, who symbolizes their sign, and they tend to know what they want and go after it with great drive and determination. They always have a well-developed sense of purpose and are not easily put off by small difficulties, or even large ones. In fact, when things are going badly the Taurian is a particularly good person to have around, because he will never panic or lose sight of important goals. He will remain solid and steady and calm.

Taurians hate to be in debt and are very careful about their financial affairs. They are intensely honest. They are not without a sense of humor, however, and they enjoy a good joke and can laugh at themselves as well. They particularly like broad slapstick comedy.

49

People born under this sign make excellent parents. They adore their children and their interest tends to center on the home and family. They also enjoy physical comfort, and Taurian women tend to be fine homemakers who combine practical good sense and artistic tendencies, expressing their good taste in interior decorating, cooking, needlework. Their homes are always warm and inviting. Both men and women are good-tempered and agreeable unless nagged and provoked, and then watch out —a Taurian will surprise you by responding like a bull who has a red flag waved in front of him.

As children, Taurians are stubborn as bulls, but they will respond to logic at a very young age and they are usually industrious in school. Singing delights Taurian children, who also often enjoy playing instruments, drawing, and painting. Children born under this sign are very affectionate and they will receive and give hugs and kisses with great enthusiasm.

Taurians do not judge people or situations in haste and they are fair and unprejudiced and peace-loving. It is pleasant to be the employee of a Taurian, because they don't fuss or nag about trivia; but don't forget, their standards are high and they expect others to be as logical, steady, and orderly as they are themselves.

Famous people born under the sign of Taurus include:

Peter Ilyich Tchaikovsky	Willie Mays
William Shakespeare	Ulysses S. Grant
Adolf Hitler	Queen Elizabeth II
Sigmund Freud	Perry Como
Harry Truman	Fred Astaire
Johann Brahms	Sugar Ray Robinson

GEMINI MAY 21–JUNE 21

People born under the sign of the twins are really always happiest when leading a double life. They are likely to have two jobs at the same time, two romances at once, a number of interesting hobbies which are quite different from one another. In personality their most noticeable characteristic is that they're changeable. They are happy one minute and sad the next, excited for a while and then very blah and deflated. They have great difficulty concentrating on one particular thing at a time. They are not at all patient and they instantly become bored with repetition in work or in play.

Gemini-born people have quick minds and they become interested in all sorts of things. They love travel, reading, meeting new people. They are adept at speed-reading, have excellent memories, and are terribly curious. They want to see new things and new places, to try new ways of doing things. They are very impatient with cautious conservative slow-moving people. Because of their active minds and their enthusiasm, Geminis seem to be ageless. They look and act "youthful" even in advanced years.

Women born under this sign are not particularly good housekeepers and their love of change and variety can make them unsuccessful marriage partners. Gemini men, too, are likely to be flirtatious and not very serious about love and marriage. Both men and women are always late, so tell a Gemini to come over at six if you really want to see him by seven.

Parents tend to worry about Gemini children who seem, from their earliest years, to be high-strung and overly active, and who flit from one project to another. They are given to temper tantrums and tearfulness. In school they often have trouble concentrating and seeing their work through, although they are generally very bright and find it easy to catch onto new things. They are restless and often described as fidgety. They learn to read easily—often at an unusually young age—and are often mechanically inclined.

Almost everyone finds the Gemini-born to be charming people with a great sense of humor, and they make particularly effective salesmen and promoters. A Gemini can sell just about anything, so be wary if you think you're being urged to buy something you really don't want. You're probably up against a smooth-talking Gemini in action.

If you are a Gemini, you may not find this news—but Geminis are particularly prone to insomnia and must guard against becoming overly fatigued.

Famous people born under the sign of Gemini include:

Jim Thorpe	Harriet Beecher Stowe
Queen Victoria	Bob Hope
Walt Whitman	Bob Dylan
John F. Kennedy	Frank Lloyd Wright
Socrates	Arthur Conan Doyle
Hubert Humphrey	Marilyn Monroe

CANCER JUNE 22–JULY 23

Cancer children are very sensitive, easily hurt by criticism, deeply attached to their parents, brothers, sisters, and friends. They themselves will make loyal and loving wives, husbands, mothers, and fathers when they are older. They tend to be sentimental and they love saving old letters, snapshots, theater programs, and school papers. They keep scrapbooks and photo albums and toys from their childhood.

People born under this sign are very emotional and they demand a good deal of approval and sympathy. Although they don't seek the spotlight, they really do want to be noticed. They do well in public roles and careers in which they have an opportunity to stimulate and teach others. Their interest in their own childhood makes them interested in other children, and they often seek opportunities to work with youngsters. They are excellent teachers.

Cancer people suffer a good deal from misunderstandings with friends or harsh discipline from parents or teachers. They are very fearful of ridicule, and therefore may be shy about showing affection or introducing ideas in classroom discussions. They can be self-conscious to an extreme, but they also tend to have considerable pride, and remember, a Cancer girl or boy never forgets an insult or an unkindness, so if you value the friendship of someone born under this sign, be careful of his feelings. He is a loyal and true friend, but he is so thin-skinned that he will worry and fret needlessly over trivial misunderstandings. Cancerians also often fear the dark, animals, loud noises. As to hobbies, Cancerians love boats, beaches, and water sports. They are good gardeners and male Cancerians are often very interested in cooking as a hobby. Photography is another popular hobby with both males and females born under this sign.

If your mother is a Cancerian, she saves all your old papers, drawings, report cards, and baby shoes—and she'll save them forever. She is not going to be particularly happy to see you grow up and become more and more independent, so you might as well be prepared. She adores you and she wants to keep you right where you are—close by her side.

Famous people born under the sign of Cancer include:

Julius Caesar	Rembrandt
Ernest Hemingway	Arthur Ashe
Ringo Starr	John Quincy Adams
Richard Rodgers	Andrew Wyeth
Phyllis Diller	John D. Rockefeller
Henry VIII	Helen Keller

LEO JULY 24–AUGUST 23

If you are a Leo you are as proud and noble as a lion, and much more friendly to other human beings! You trust others, never hold a grudge, and are willing to work hard.

Leo people are strong and ambitious and Leo boys are always ready for a fight, whether it be an actual boxing or wrestling exercise or an argument or debate. Leos are self-confident and often tend to be boastful. There are no shy Leos. They are brave in the face of danger and they demand success for themselves. Failure is even harder for the Leo to accept than it is for most other people.

A Leo can often become very unhappy if he does not see results immediately from his ambitious undertakings. Also, since Leos always want to make the rules in everything they take part in, they are frequently frustrated and angry when others take over. They may try to get their way by force or by persuasion, but in either case they do not give in easily. Women who are Leos often dominate their husbands, but since they are very generous and high-minded they may put their energies instead into good works and all sorts of community projects. Most Leos want praise so badly that they tend to show off a bit too much, but if they are careful to avoid this their leadership and charm will make them very popular socially. An interesting thing about people born under Leo is that they are boastful not only about their own achievements but those of their families, because they believe that anything that belongs to them—like a father or a sister—is really the very best in the whole world.

Leos love to teach and often grow up to be educators. As children Leos are leaders of the gang. They are also generous and jolly—as long as they get their own way. They love being asked to speak in front of the class. They love spending money and going to parties—and they hate doing chores around the house.

Famous people born under the sign of Leo include:

Napoleon Bonaparte	Fidel Castro
Henry Ford	Jacqueline Kennedy Onassis
Benito Mussolini	Ogden Nash
Percy Bysshe Shelley	Lucille Ball
Mae West	George Bernard Shaw
Alfred Hitchcock	Julia Child

VIRGO AUGUST 24–SEPTEMBER 23

People born under the sign of Virgo are methodical, intelligent, and practical. They are intelligent people who write well, are good critics of art and literature, have fine memories, and are particularly successful in the sort of schoolwork that requires careful research and organization. Virgo-born boys and girls are much gentler and more reserved than Aries or Leo people, and unlike the Aries or Leos they enjoy detailed work and don't mind routine and repetition.

People born under this sign are willing to work hard at keeping books and records in order. They are excellent as class secretaries or treasurers, and can always be trusted to keep accounts with great accuracy and neatness. Since their standards are so high they really don't want anyone to assist them. They much prefer to take care of things alone. Virgo-born people do not seek the highest leadership positions, but are content to work away quietly without much notice. They are modest people and they like being alone.

Basically, the Virgo man or woman is intellectual rather than emotional. He is often critical of people who are not his sort, and his criticism can hurt others and make them angry and irritable with him if they are frequently thrown together in a family, school, or work situation. Actually, he is not very sensitive to other people's feelings and, although he means well and tries to be helpful, he often forgets to praise others when they deserve it or to behave sympathetically to friends when they are troubled. He must be careful to avoid trying to make over friends and relatives whose personalities are not like his.

Young Virgos are fussy eaters and rather bashful. They are excellent mimics. They are efficient and dependable in school from first grade on and they enjoy helping the teacher. As teen-agers they are often self-conscious and don't appreciate teasing one bit. They are almost always helpful at home and they manage money wisely.

Famous people born under the sign of Virgo include:

Christopher Columbus	Greta Garbo
Arthur Godfrey	Peter Sellers
Alexander the Great	O. Henry
Sophia Loren	William Howard Taft
Leonard Bernstein	Queen Elizabeth I
Lafayette	Leo Tolstoi

LIBRA SEPTEMBER 24–OCTOBER 23

Libra-born men and women are artistic, sympathetic, and kind. They are genuine peace-makers because they themselves like living in harmony with others. They love beauty, appreciate art and music a great deal, are fussy about their clothing. You will find that they are very tidy, and that they dislike mess and disorder and rebel against any task that they consider "dirty work." They hate confusion and commotion.

People born when the sun is in Libra are very courteous, and they dislike bad manners in others. Their interest in perfection can make them extremely painstaking about detail. They dislike ugliness in any form and are very sensitive to the beauties of nature. They like people but they hate crowds. They are very intelligent and are almost always attractive-looking with particularly nice smiles. However, they often have to watch their weight, and tend to worry unnecessarily about their health.

Love is terribly important to the Libran and frequently these people marry very young. They tend to be very popular with the opposite sex from their early teens until old age. Actually, they make better husbands and wives than they do parents, because, although they take good care of their children, their whole world tends to center on their marriage partner.

Although Librans are basically artistic they may also be very clever in business, and they often become quite wealthy. The well-balanced Libra mind sees both sides of a question and weighs them to see which is the most valuable. Many people rely on a Libra friend to help them in making important decisions, and they are right to do so. It is thought that many Librans are psychic because their intuitions seem so frequently to be correct.

Libra children hate being pushed to make a decision and they also hate being rushed. They are charming and bright and often become teachers' pets. They show the Libran tidiness very early and they are also likely to enjoy music and art. As teen-agers they are very interested in romance and always have a special girl-friend or boyfriend—although it may be a different one every week.

Famous people born under the sign of Libra include:

Mohandas Gandhi	Noah Webster
William Penn	Truman Capote
David Ben-Gurion	Mickey Mantle
Charlie Brown	John Lennon
Eugene O'Neill	Dwight D. Eisenhower
Brigitte Bardot	Al Capp

SCORPIO OCTOBER 24–NOVEMBER 22

Scorpios are energetic and forceful. They like to work hard, and they are very independent. Furthermore, they're really pretty cool characters. They use their wiles and their wits to accomplish their aims and they persevere until they get what they want.

People born under Scorpio are particularly good at keeping secrets, and they like strenuous activity, roughing it, competing energetically in difficult sports. Sometimes Scorpios are poor sports and bad losers and may even be dishonest in games because they are so intent on winning. At home they can be extremely severe and demanding of others.

In love, Scorpios are very devoted with the same sort of intense devotion they can give to their work or to good causes. However, if their affection is not returned they will lose interest quickly.

It's strange that while Scorpios are very critical of others, they really hate to be criticized themselves. They must guard against their tendency to be overly critical and should learn to understand and appreciate the people with whom they work and live.

Scorpios are very good at fixing things, skillful with their hands, and original in their work. They are heroic, and even as very young children they show this quality. They enjoy privacy, and Scorpio children often keep diaries and prefer desks they can lock. They love frightening movies and scary television shows and ghost stories.

Women born under this sign often rebel against the restrictions put on their sex. They either wish they had been born male or go into more typically male pursuits than women born under other signs. They may become very active in women's rights movements. They are strong and efficient and bold and are not very tolerant of weaker, less capable women.

Both male and female Scorpios have trouble understanding any viewpoint but their own. They can argue for hours, trying to make sure they get the last word. Scorpios simply hate to compromise so you'd better just give up trying to make a Scorpio friend come to an agreement with you. *You're* going to have to be the one to give in.

Famous people born under the sign of Scorpio include:

Daniel Boone	Pablo Picasso
Richard Burton	Chiang Kai-Shek
Marie Curie	Charles de Gaulle
Robert Kennedy	Jonas Salk
Johnny Carson	Marie Antoinette
Mike Nichols	Leon Trotsky

SAGITTARIUS NOVEMBER 23–DECEMBER 21

If you are a Sagittarian you love debate and have discovered that you can often sway people to your point of view with your arguments. You are clever in ordinary conversation as well and you often hold people entranced at parties with your jokes and stories.

Another notable feature of Sagittarians is that they tend to be sports-lovers, both as participants and as observers. They like the country and their favorite sport is often horseback riding or hunting or fishing.

Like the Libran, the Sagittarian has frequent strong intuitions and is more likely than people born under many other signs to have extrasensory perception. Sagittarians trust their intuitions and instincts and seem to do best when they act on them.

The Sagittarian, like the symbol of his sign, is as direct as a well-aimed arrow. He is honest and loyal, informal and friendly, unselfish and idealistic. He may not be very tactful, because he hates shading the truth in any way. He is particularly scornful of untruthfulness in others. Because of this bluntness he will not court a woman in a romantic poetic fashion, and the Sagittarian woman will also lack flirtatiousness and artifice. Sometimes the result of this honesty is lack of diplomacy which may cause Sagittarians problems with their friends and business associates. They are often totally frank when it really would be better not to be.

Sagittarian children are endlessly curious, seem to talk continuously, and are extremely active physically. They hate stuffy places and always want to play out in the open air. They are attracted to danger, as are Sagittarian adults, and are extremely daring. They are also extravagant with money and enjoy gambling, but this rarely develops into a serious problem. Sagittarian boys and girls like school, particularly when given the freedom to work at their own pace.

Famous people born under the sign of Sagittarius include:

Winston Churchill	James Thurber
Frank Sinatra	Sammy Davis, Jr.
Mark Twain	Jane Fonda
Maria Callas	John Lindsay
Joe DiMaggio	Ludwig van Beethoven
John Milton	Walt Disney

CAPRICORN DECEMBER 22–JANUARY 20

The Capricornian is likely to be a rather conservative responsible fellow who upholds authority, takes a practical approach to most matters, and is not very romantic or sentimental. The Capricorn-born feel that they know what is morally right and what is wrong, and they will work very hard to uphold traditional standards. People born under this sign are anxious to get ahead. They actively seek material success and a rise in social status, and they often achieve both. They respect other people whom they consider successful. They drive a hard bargain and even if they have money, they may be miserly. They are also cautious and they tend to worry about the future and about failure.

When a man or woman born under this sign becomes a parent, he or she does not value self-expression and imagination in children as much as obedience and a sense of responsibility. Capricornians tend to be strong disciplinarians. Capricorn children are strong-willed, orderly about their possessions, and well-organized about their school work. They can, however, be terribly stubborn and bossy.

Oddly, Capricornians are very prone to depression, and often they take to drink or drugs. It is thought that their lack of natural high spirits causes them to seek artificial stimulation. Despite their lack of gaiety, however, they are excellent hosts who love entertaining, particularly on family occasions.

Like the goat climbing up a mountain, people born under this sign pursue an upward course unswervingly. Even as children they are very serious about schoolwork and responsibilities at home. They are likely to take on part-time jobs as soon as they are old enough. They like to manage and persuade others, and may consider themselves authorities on how to act and how to dress. They can be a bit overbearing and also, unfortunately, a bit snobbish.

A mother born under the sign of Capricorn will teach her children to be respectful, thrifty, and well-mannered. She is not particularly demonstrative, but she is definitely devoted, even though she may seem strict and a bit too serious toward youngsters.

Famous people born under the sign of Capricorn include:

Martin Luther King	Muhammad Ali
Richard Nixon	Clara Barton
Edgar Allan Poe	Joseph Stalin
Barry Goldwater	Isaac Newton
Benjamin Franklin	Artur Rubinstein
Humphrey Bogart	Pablo Casals

AQUARIUS JANUARY 21–FEBRUARY 19

The finest characteristics of the Aquarian-born are their broad vision, open-mindedness, and lack of prejudice. They may be described as noble, wise, tolerant of others. They don't try to run other people's lives and they are not critical of others who are different from themselves. They believe in justice and freedom with complete sincerity.

Aquarians are internationalists who believe in the brotherhood of man and the brotherhood of nations. You should always pick an Aquarian if you want someone to judge a disagreement, because they are so fair.

Aquarian parents are reasonable and gentle. They are neither too severe nor too lax. They try to teach their children the same fairness, helpfulness, moderation, and interest in freedom that they hold dear. Aquarian children are often absent-minded but delightful boys and girls who enjoy new activities and have many different interests and hobbies. They tend to decide on a career early in life, and often it's a very unusual one.

Since Aquarians are soft-spoken people they may not be immediately recognized as leaders, but in fact they are marvelous in positions of responsibility. They are even-tempered and calm and they attack problems logically and systematically, but they are also imaginative and inventive. They make friends slowly, but they remain thereafter eternally loyal. They are fascinated with politics, sports, young children and the elderly, clocks and watches, automobiles.

Strangely, Aquarians have poor memories and also have problems with their power of concentration. They are also rather cautious physically, and as children they may be teased because of their fear of rough games or difficult sports. They also often fear planes and elevators. However, they are *not* fearful of other people's opinions.

Aquarians live in accordance with their ideals, but they rarely fight to the finish for a cause they believe in. They simply are idealists but not fighters. They find unpleasantness, arguments, shouting, and discord very distasteful, and when a loud debate begins they often depart.

If you want to borrow money, don't ask an Aquarian. He may *give* you the shirt from his back, but he dislikes lending and borrowing. Aquarians don't use charge accounts and credit cards very happily and like to pay as they go whenever possible.

Famous people born under the sign of Aquarius include:

Abraham Lincoln	Wolfgang Amadeus Mozart
Babe Ruth	Charles Darwin
W. C. Fields	Franklin D. Roosevelt
Adlai Stevenson	Paul Newman
Thomas Edison	Galileo
Charles Dickens	Mia Farrow

PISCES FEBRUARY 20–MARCH 21

The Piscean person has very little ambition for social prestige, financial gain, or public acclaim. He is a gentle, dreamy, sometimes melancholy type, who like the Capricornian may be inclined to alcohol and drug addiction.

Pisceans are idealistic folk who can be extremely lazy and impractical. They are self-sacrificing and devoted to others. They are also quite gullible, always believing what others tell them and trusting that it is correct. Sometimes they are unwisely generous to people who do not appreciate their goodness and take advantage of them.

People born under Pisces love natural beauty as well as art. They are often quite talented and, although they are not by nature competitive, they may reach professional status in an artistic field, particularly in acting.

Despite this fact, Pisceans lack self-confidence and most of them don't work well alone. They tend to be rather nervous and anxious about starting new ventures. They are physically restless and as schoolchildren are often criticized for inattentiveness. They enjoy solitude and meditation and their lack of worldly ambition can occasionally result in a life of aimless drifting.

As young children they are highly imaginative and they demand constant attention. Many Pisces children love music and dancing and poetry. Like Pisces adults, they are moody, sentimental, and basically shy, and although they may learn to act with greater confidence as they grow up, they really prefer to stay away from competitive situations. By the way, Pisceans have a terrible time keeping a secret.

The Piscean is a nonconformist and may have trouble in school learning through the routine methods. He enjoys literature, particularly poetry, and often finds math impossible. He likes to write and may be gifted in this direction. His understanding of other people's problems and sufferings makes him a truly sympathetic friend. Pisceans cry easily, both as children and as adults, and are excellent listeners.

Famous people born under the sign of Pisces include:

Frederic Chopin	George Washington
Michelangelo	Harry Belafonte
Elizabeth Taylor	Sidney Poitier
Grover Cleveland	John Steinbeck
Albert Einstein	Auguste Renoir
Rudolf Nureyev	Enrico Caruso

3

Palmistry

When we look into a person's hand to study his character and see into his future we are practicing an ancient method of fortune-telling, believed to have been known four thousand years ago in China, Egypt, Babylonia, and Chaldea. The earliest *written* accounts, however, are in Greek, from which we derive another name for palmistry—chiromancy.

Reading palms has always been a favorite gypsy fortune-telling method. The gypsies are believed to have come originally from India, where there were written records of astrology and hand reading at least as early as the third century B.C. Well before that, in the sixth century B.C., Buddha was recognized as a holy man at birth by the markings on his soles and palms. The Old Testament has many references to the commonly held idea that man's fate can be found inscribed in his hands. Perhaps the best known is from Proverbs 3:16: "Length of days is in her right hand; and in her left hand riches and honor." Palmistry spread from the Near East throughout Europe in the Middle Ages, and has been a subject of considerable interest right up to contemporary times.

One of the signs of Buddha's special mission was the strange marking in his palm, which was noticed at his birth. The seated figure, made of dry lacquer, is Chinese and dates from the Yuan dynasty in the thirteenth century. The standing Buddha is Indian, from the second or third century A.D., and shows Buddha raising his hand in a gesture which gives freedom from fear.

Palm reading is only one technique—and the most popular by far—of learning about a person by studying bodily signs. All such techniques are based on the belief that the outer form, the body, is a reflection of the inner form, the personality. Physiognomists study the face, the shape, and the bearing of their subject; phrenologists examine the bumps and depressions of the skull. In China there is an old tradition of podoscopy—the practice of reading the markings on the bottoms of the feet. Hospitals footprint newborn infants today because these prints, like fingerprints, are absolutely unique and serve as positive identification.

Reading palms can be a fascinating hobby, at once simple and intricate. Its simplicity lies in the fact that all that is needed is two people in a serious inquiring frame of mind. Its complexity lies in the endless variation of palm markings found in different hands. We speak of "reading" a hand because these unique markings are considered symbols, like the letters of the alphabet, which are inscribed on our hands as writing is inscribed on a page. After you learn what these symbols mean, you can then "read" what is "written." The markings on the palm may also be thought of as a road map that shows where you have been and where you are going.

Once you have learned the basic rules of palmistry, you will be able to discover these things about your subject:

1. His talents and abilities. These are personality traits he was born with, the characteristics he inherited from his parents.
2. How he has developed these abilities; in other words, what sort of person he actually is at this time.
3. What the future holds in store for him.

If you begin by reading your own palm first you may be in for some startling surprises. If you then examine the palms of the other members of your family, you may change your mind completely about the traits you inherited from your mother or your father, and whether you are more like your sister or your brother.

Whether we trust that the future is in our palms or not, most

An early palmistry book. Note the astrological symbols used to designate areas of the hand.

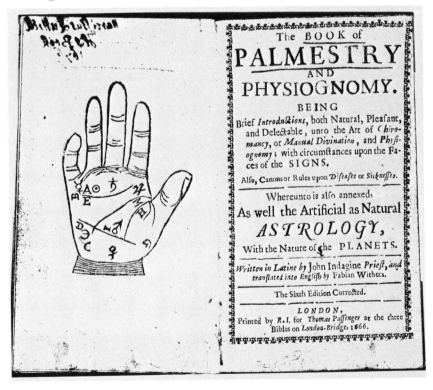

of us do believe that hands reveal a good deal about personality. We expect pianists to have "artistic hands"—long and slender and well shaped. We judge a woman to be helpless if she has tiny fluttery hands. If her hands are square and strong we may draw the conclusion that she is unusually capable. Actors and actresses use their hands with great skill to help convey the personality of the characters they are depicting. Doctors gain definite medical impressions about a person by looking at his hands in a physical examination to see if the nails are bitten, if the color of the skin and nails is pale, whether the hands are moist or dry, cold or hot.

When you start reading palms, you don't have to be a seer or a gypsy fortune-teller to look at a pair of perfectly smooth hands with beautifully manicured nails and decide that this is someone who is concerned about his looks and who doesn't earn his living digging ditches. At the opposite extreme, if your subject stretches out grimy hands covered with cuts and bruises and callouses, marked by bitten and broken fingernails, you will undoubtedly be correct in assuming that he engages in manual labor and is not fastidiously interested in his physical appearance. Most people do not, of course, present striking cases of this sort, so proceed slowly and with caution.

You will not be surprised to find that, since fortune-tellers believe that the same fate is inscribed for you on your palm and in the stars, certain signs in the hand are named after signs in the heavens. There are close relationships in the development of the arts of astrology and palmistry through the ages.

HOW TO MAKE PALM PRINTS

Some palm readers like to make palm prints both as an aid in reading the lines in the palm and as a record for comparison with other hands. You will find palm prints particularly useful for comparing the hands of the members of your family. Like finger-prints, palm prints are made by inking the hand and then press-ing it down on a piece of paper. Use a cloth-covered stamping pad and ink the inside of your hand, including fingers and thumbs, by pressing each area against the pad. You must start with clean dry hands and ink about a quarter of your hand at a time. Use a corner of the ink pad to get at the hollow in the cen-ter of your palm. Then press your hand down in the center of a piece of smooth white paper. Make a number of prints and select the set in which the lines show up most clearly. You must have a print of each hand. You should also make a tracing of the gen-eral outline of the hand, placing the hand on a piece of paper in a natural position and holding the pencil straight up and down to get an accurate outline. You may also make palm prints by putting linoleum-print ink on your hand, just as you would on a block, by first rolling it out on a piece of glass. If your palm is very high in the center put a piece of folded cloth or rubber under the paper in this area to press it up against your hand when making your print. Be careful not to ink too heavily or you will fill in the lines. The stamping pad is easier to work with for this reason.

Remember:
1. The shape of your hand shows a general approach to life.
2. The mounts of the hand tell where your energy lies and how it is being used.
3. The lines in the hand give indication of where you are headed. It is for this reason that the lines in the hand are said to change as you, yourself, direct your destiny.

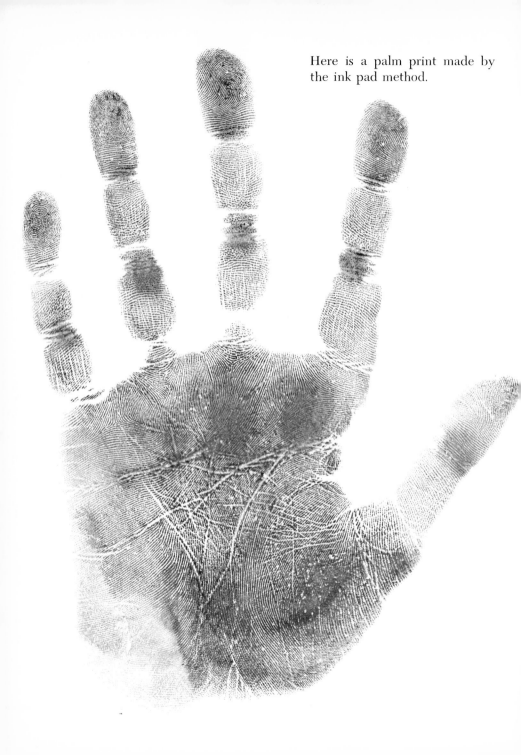

Here is a palm print made by the ink pad method.

EXAMINATION OF THE ENTIRE HAND

According to the rules set down by a fourteenth-century expert, a palm should be read between meals—never just after or just before. The hand should also be pleasantly warm, not too hot or too cold. It is stated that heat and cold dull the lines of the palm as does a very full or a very empty stomach.

In a dignified and serious manner take the subject's two hands in yours and first note their size. If the hand is large in proportion to the body this is probably an intelligent person who also has the ability to do detailed work with his hands. Many dentists have this type of hand; so do many pickpockets. If the hand is short in proportion to the body, expect to find that the person makes hasty judgments, is immature, quick-tempered, likely to be a gossip. This is a poor type of person to select for class president or committee chairman, for instance, because he or she becomes bored easily, and although he enjoys making plans he may neglect to carry them out. A correctly proportioned hand should be the same length from the wrist to the top of the middle finger as the face is from the tip of the chin to the hairline.

Here is another way to measure. If the palm is as broad as it is long, this is considered a broad hand. A small hand in an adult woman is any hand less than 6¾″ long; under 7″ is a small man's hand. Very broad hands indicate drive and physical energy and are often found on people who have good common sense, are generous and tolerant, and finish jobs once they start them. Exceptionally narrow hands indicate nervous energy, a more inward turn of mind, lack of sympathy toward others, and a person who tends to be shy and whose feelings are easily hurt.

After you have made these observations take the subject's hand in yours and try to bend the fingers back. A flexible hand is a sign of a flexible mind. In a very flexible hand the fingers can be

73

bent back almost at right angles to the hand itself. If the fingers are so stiff that they won't bend back at all, expect this to be someone who never changes his mind and who is also rather miserly. If you are examining the hand of your aged neighbor or your great-grandmother, remember that stiffness of the hands is very common in older people and may not indicate anything about personality.

Now ask the subject to place his hands in a natural position on the table, palms downward. If the fingers are placed close together it indicates a cautious and conventional personality; if wide apart, a quick and imaginative mind. Look at the fingers. Short fingers are a sign of impulsiveness; long fingers indicate that the subject has trouble making decisions. If the ring finger is longer than the index finger the subject can expect generally good luck except in money matters. A *very* short index finger indicates feelings of inferiority, but if the opposite is true expect him to be a pleasure lover and a financial success. An index finger that is *quite* a bit longer than the ring finger is indication that the person is very bossy and domineering. If it is longer than the middle finger it indicates a tyrant or a dictator. Adolf Hitler is believed to have had this sign.

Look at the color of the hands. Very white hands may indicate disease or nervousness. If, however, the hands before you look unusually rosy, they are likely to belong to someone with an optimistic and loving nature.

Now look at the general shape of the hands, making a tracing if you find this helpful, and compare them to these diagrams. The shape of the hand is thought, by palmists, to directly reflect the person's general approach to life. It is an extremely important aspect of the total reading. In judging whether fingers are long or short notice that *no* one's fingers are longer than his palm. Fingers that look extremely long will usually be found equally as long as—or almost as long as—the palm. Average length means the middle finger is about as long as the back of the hand from knuckles to wrist.

THE SEVEN BASIC HAND SHAPES

1. The elemental hand
2. The square hand
3. The spatulate hand
4. The artistic hand
5. The philosophical hand
6. The pointed hand
7. Mixed hands, combining two or more of any of the above classifications.

ELEMENTAL HAND

This is the hand that is clumsy, rigid, and thick, with a broad palm and a short thumb. There are few lines on the palm and the skin is coarse. This hand type is associated with people who are doers rather than thinkers—conservative, slow, and materialistic. Frankly, this is not a desirable hand type, because it is also associated with primitive behavior and poor intelligence.

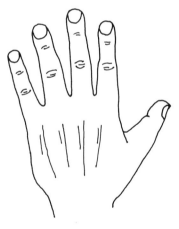

SQUARE HAND

This is a much more common shape than the true elemental hand. The square hand has a palm which looks square at the wrist or the base of the fingers. The nails are short and square in shape. People with this hand type tend to be punctual and methodical. They are tidy in their habits and set great store by appearance. They are law-abiding citizens who concentrate on one thing at a time, and who usually prefer what is useful to what is beautiful if they have to make such a choice. They are sincere and good friends, as you may already have discovered.

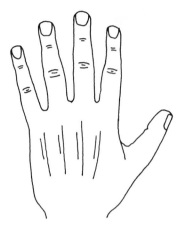

SPATULATE HAND

This hand is shaped rather like a spade. The fingers are somewhat flat and flare out on either side of the nails making them wider at the tip than at the base. They do not have big joints, however, and the entire hand tends to be rather smooth. People with this type of hand are original thinkers with advanced ideas, who are usually described as being ahead of their time. They are impatient but optimistic, self-confident, and energetic. These people may be geniuses or they may be kooks. In any case, they always stand out as being different from the crowd.

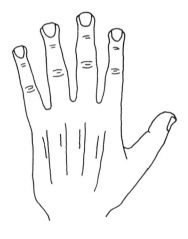

CONIC OR ARTISTIC HANDS

Conic hands have fingers that are full at the base and taper toward the ends. The palm in this hand type also tapers. People with conic hands adore admiration. They simply can't live without love. They tend to be impatient folk who seek luxury and beauty in their surroundings and who are, unfortunately, not careful to carry out their always-good intentions. They lack physical energy and may turn toward melancholy.

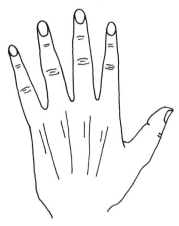

THE PHILOSOPHICAL HAND

This is a long-fingered hand with knotty joints and a large angular look, which often goes with a long bony body. People with this hand type use their hands in talking and often grow long nails. These are analytical folk who love to discuss and debate. They are interested in searching out truth and they often view themselves as life-long students. They also may be quite egotistical. Some people with this hand shape have a great need for solitude and they may turn to mysticism.

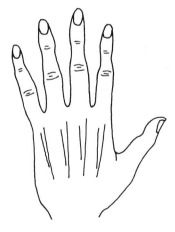

THE POINTED HAND

This is the type of hand which most people consider extremely beautiful. Models in nail polish ads have this hand type. It is delicately shaped, with slender tapering fingers, and it looks fragile, although it is found on plump people as well as on those who are slight in build. People who have pointed hands are gentle and quiet. They lack business sense and have no feeling for punctuality. They are unaggressive and unambitious. These people live in a world of dreams and ideals, are attracted to mystery and magic, and are often highly intuitive.

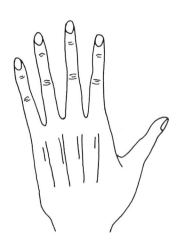

THE MIXED HAND

Most people do not have hands that fit precisely into one of the above categories. Sometimes hands are truly mixed —with fingers which are quite different in shape from one another, palms that are broad with fingers that are narrow, etc. Try to fit the hand you are examining into the category it most easily matches, but if it is a true jumble of characteristics, it is to be considered a mixed hand and a sign of energy, versa-

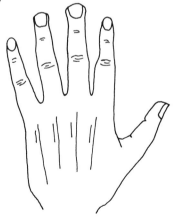

78

tility, and adaptability. People with mixed hands are good at many things, often have more than one career, and are very involved with a number of hobbies, sports, and community affairs.

MOUNTS OF THE HAND

In palmistry each finger has a name and the fleshy pad below each finger is its "mount." The influence of astrology is seen in the naming of these landmarks, and it is believed that if Saturn, for example, has a powerful position in your horoscope, the finger and mount of Saturn will show a similar development and importance in your hand, indicating the same influences in your personality.

Look at this map of the mounts of the hand and then examine the base of your fingers and try to determine which of these hills and valleys in your own hand are large and which are small. High padding of the mounts in general indicates considerable energy. Rather soft padding is indicative of *intellectual* rather than physical energy. Nearly flat mounts indicate nervous energy or lack of forcefulness.

Check your hand print for the little lines on the mounts. A number of tiny lines on a mount shows lack of control and indicates that you may have been using the qualities of the mount poorly. One clear line or a few strong markings on a mount indicate that the qualities associated with that mount are being well used.

MOUNT OF VENUS

This mount at the base of the thumb is the large thick area sometimes referred to, with the Mount of the Moon, as the "heel" of the hand. A very large Mount of Venus confers the Venus-like qualities of affection, warmth, generosity, and success in love. Desire for admiration may be the weak point of a person with a large Mount of Venus, but in general these people are genuinely lovable, so it's no problem. They are also noted for good taste in color, in music, and in art. If there is virtually no mount, this is someone with a cold withdrawn personality.

MOUNT OF JUPITER

The Mount of Jupiter, at the base of the index finger, is associated with a healthy degree of pride, ambition, and the desire for power. Overdevelopment indicates a dictator or an overwhelmingly ambitious and egotistical person. An extremely small Mount of Jupiter is found on people who are lazy and vulgar and utterly lacking in dignity.

MOUNT OF SATURN

This mount at the base of the middle finger, if normally developed, shows a sound, trustworthy, and rather cautious person. If it is very large it is a sign of moodiness, melancholy, and love of solitude. Its absence simply shows very run-of-the-mill abilities and limited talents.

MOUNT OF APOLLO or MOUNT OF THE SUN

A normally developed Mount of Apollo is a sign of good luck, good taste, artistic ability, optimism, and imagination. If there is no mount below this finger it indicates the opposite—lack of any feeling for art or beauty, coldness, pessimism. If overly devel-

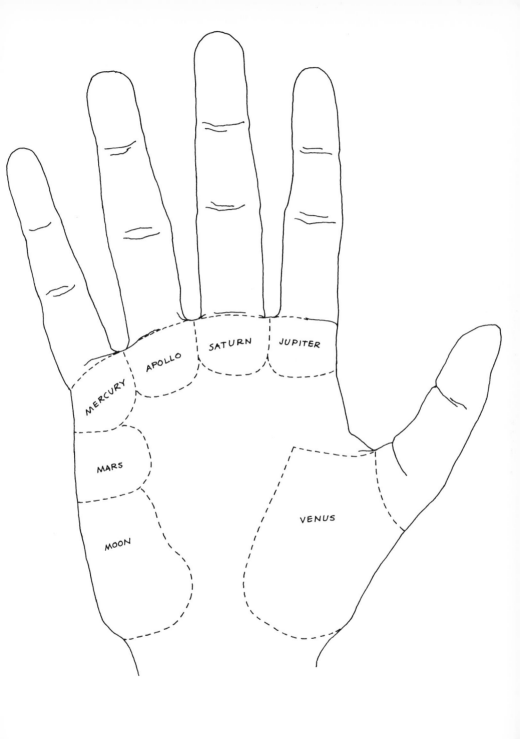

oped, this is a person who is boastful, who loves publicity and show. Such people are pretentious and avid for money and overrate their own abilities.

MOUNT OF MERCURY

This is the mount beneath the little finger, and it is well marked in people who are intelligent, witty, and quick-thinking. People with this sign love change, travel, and excitement, and they tend to choose work that permits this sort of variety. Unfortunately, too much development of this mount indicates a person who lies, cheats, and conducts business matters unscrupulously. A very small Mount of Mercury is found on people who are dreadful bores—humorless and long-winded.

MOUNT OF MARS

This mount is on the outer edge of the hand below the Mount of Mercury. It indicates courage and self-control, but if it is very large it shows aggressiveness and often criminal violence. No visible mount or a very small mount is the mark of the coward.

MOUNT OF THE MOON

The Mount of the Moon is below the Mount of Mars on the outer part of the palm near the wrist. This mount controls the gentle qualities of sentiment and imagination. A normally developed Mount of the Moon is found on people who are romantic and sensitive, who like literature and art and may be gifted in these areas. If there is excessive development of this mount, this is someone who is touchy—quick to take offense and a prey to imaginary illnesses. If the mount is flat the person is inflexible and may be a troublemaker as well. Occult powers are shown when this mount is very highly developed toward the wrist.

LINES OF THE HAND

There are a great many lines in the hand and their variations are the most fascinating aspect of palm reading. When you do hand prints the tiny lines show up much more clearly than when examined with the naked eye. You might also try looking at your hand through a magnifying glass and you'll be amazed at the amount of detail you will see. A richly lined hand is taken to indicate a thinking person rather than a man (or woman) of action! Note in the section on hand shapes that the elemental hand has few lines.

Generally the lines in one hand differ from those in the other, and the most used hand (usually the right) will be the better marked. In medieval days the left hand was read because it is closest to the heart and the heart was considered to be the center of personality. Now we examine both hands—the left for inherited characteristics and the right for the present psychological make-up. The comparison is always interesting, but the right hand is considered the more important in a reading. In a left-handed person, however, the process must be reversed. You may be able to astonish a stranger by correctly telling him whether he is right- or left-handed. To do this, look for telltale signs—a "writer's bump" on the middle finger, or the presence of other thickenings and callouses on the more used hand. Also, the fingers may be noticeably larger on this hand. You have probably noticed this yourself when trying a ring on one ring finger and then on the other. If the lines on both hands are almost identical, it indicates a less interesting life and personality than if they differ markedly.

A "good hand" has lines which are clear, narrow, sharp, and

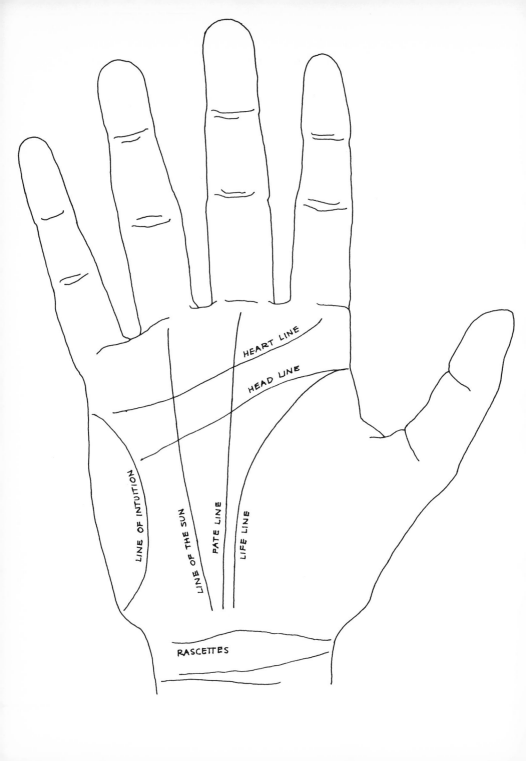

HEART LINE

HEAD LINE

LINE OF INTUITION

LINE OF THE SUN

PATE LINE

LIFE LINE

RASCETTES

free of breaks. Chained lines—these really look like a series of tiny links—and are a weak sign, and breaks in lines indicate failure. Lines which are forked at the end, except in the case of the life line, give greater power to the force of that line in your life. Lines rising from a major horizontal line toward the fingers accentuate its influence, and lines falling from it toward the wrist weaken it. If you see a clear triangle formed by the head, life, and fate lines, this is an extremely lucky hand. If it also has mounts which are neither excessively flat nor unusually high and straight fingers and is a flexible hand, a happy life is almost certain. A "bad hand" has twisted fingers, lines that are twisted and broken in many places, very uneven development of mounts or no development at all. This hand means trouble, particularly if it also has small thumbs, showing lack of willpower.

The major lines are the life line, head line, and heart line. Other important lines include the line of fate, the line of the sun, the line of intuition, and the wrist lines, or rascettes.

Read the lines of the right hand unless your subject is left-handed.

LIFE LINE

The life line relates to energy and not simply to length of life. Many people have been cruelly frightened when readers have observed their life lines and predicted early death. A long, narrow, and deep line without irregularities or breaks is considered a promise of long life, good health, and great strength and energy. If, however, the line is short, irregular, and interrupted, it often means that this person will live by his wits rather than by his physical strength. A broken line may indicate frequent illnesses or generally low energy levels. Where the life line joins the head line, look at the angle they form. If the angle is less than 45°, the person will be a good businessman or woman. If the life line and head line are joined for as much as a third of the length of the head line it indicates timidity. If the two lines don't meet it may indicate that this person doesn't get along well with others, and often this sign is found on a man or woman who is vain or boastful. A life line that looks rather like a chain at the start and becomes a more distinct line indicates frail health in childhood followed by robust health as an adult. Lines which droop downward from the life line are travel lines. When the life line forks at the bottom you are looking at a person who will travel a long distance and perhaps go to live in another country. If your life line, instead of curving round the Mount of Venus, goes diagonally across your hand, passing close to the Mount of the Moon, you are a very restless person, a lover of action and demanding sports. If, however, the line curves closely around the thumb, it shows a preference for mental rather than physical exertion.

HEAD LINE

If your head line only slopes slightly it indicates practicality and love of possessions and luxuries. However, if it slopes sharply downward toward the wrist, it shows imagination and sensitivity. Often the head line and the life line begin together, and this indicates that you will find shrewd business sense. When this is not so, it means that the person is bold, impulsive, independent, quick to make decisions and to act. If the space between the two lines is great, the subject will be overly rash, foolish, careless. If the head line is very straight across the hand and curves slightly upward, it means that this person is cold and logical and will become wealthy. He will also be a severe taskmaster who expects hard work of his employees and associates. If the line is so short that it ends at the middle of the hand, this subject completely lacks imagination and has a rather dull one-track mind. If it is also linked—made up of chainlike pieces—it shows indecision. If there is very little space between the head line and the heart line, the head will rule the heart when the head line is the deeper and stronger line—and the heart will rule the head if the opposite is true. Some palmists believe that insanity is predicted in a hand that shows a head line sinking very sharply down into the Mount of the Moon, and toward the center of the wrist. A strong, sharply etched head line indicates high intelligence and great powers of concentration, regardless of personality makeup. If the head line forks at the end, with one fork approaching the heart line and the other sloping down toward the Mount of the Moon, you are examining the hand of a person who will sacrifice anything for love. If the fork comes at the end of a long sloping head line it shows talent for self-expression, particularly in the areas of writing and acting. If the head line on the right hand is much longer than that on the left, it indicates a self-made man or woman who has worked hard and done the most with his capabilities, despite lack of opportunities in childhood.

HEART LINE

The heart line and head line must be studied together because, as stated earlier in talking about the head line, the question of whether the head or the heart rules the person's nature is shown by the relative positions of these lines. Chained heart lines are very common and indicate emotional people who are subject to "ups" and "downs." If the line of the heart begins at the Mount of Jupiter it shows deep enduring affections, but when it begins at the Mount of Saturn, the person is likely to have many love affairs and to be unfaithful in marriage. When it begins with a fork on the Mount of Jupiter it is a particularly strong indication of happy marriage—showing an honest enthusiastic lover whose devotion is deep and faithful. The hand prints of monkeys and gorillas show the so-called simian line—a single horizontal line representing both the head and heart lines which have run together. About 6 percent of human beings have a simian line. If you find this line in a palm you are reading, think twice before saying so. It is said that a larger percentage of people with this sign turn out to be criminals. However, another large group of people with simian hands are found to be particularly gifted and also intensely religious. Watch out what you predict for someone with this astonishing palm sign. If the line of the heart runs across the entire hand, from side to side, it indicates great—or too great—affection, leading to jealousy. A short heart line, however, is a sign of the selfish ungiving personality. Look for a very small line above the heart line on the edge of the Mount of Mercury. This is the line of marriage, and if there is more than one consider yourself warned.

LINE OF FATE

A long well-defined line of fate going from the Mount of Saturn to the wrist indicates success, fame, and fortune. This line relates to the people who influence your career and, in general, to all matters affecting power, ambition, the accumulation of wealth. When it is broken and uneven it shows that there will be successes and failures, an uneven course of events. A total break in the line is thought to be a definite sign of important changes due to loss and calamity. Lines crossing the fate line are obstacles in the route. A good clear long fate line generally shows strength of purpose in all periods of life, as well as high social position. The length of this line can vary enormously, and it is totally absent from about one in every five hands. However, many young children without this line develop one before the age of twenty. The lack of a fate line is generally taken to mean that you must work very hard to achieve success. If the fate line starts inside the life line rather than up under the middle finger, it shows that success in life will come through family help and influence. If it starts in the center of the palm it shows success by your own efforts.

LINE OF THE SUN

If your hand shows this vertical sign, going from the Mount of Apollo to the wrist or part of the way, you may consider yourself very lucky. If you have a good fate line as well, you are even more favored. A sharp sun line accompanied by a sloping head line indicates talent in poetry and literature and a very artistic nature in general. This is the symbol of self-expression and self-realization. There is no assurance of material gain, but every indication of fulfillment of abilities and spiritual gratification.

LINE OF INTUITION

This semicircular line, which curls around the Mount of Mars and extends down into the Mount of the Moon, is only found on the hands of people with sixth sense. It is a more common mark on the hands of women than on the hands of men. If you scored high in the ESP tests in the first chapter, take a magnifying glass to your palms and see if you have the secret sign, the line of intuition.

RASCETTES

These are the three bracelets that you find below the palm, circling the wrist. If sharp and straight, these lines indicate wealth and good health, although if they are chainlike it indicates that hard work and ambition will be required to achieve this financial state. If the lines are faint and wavy they warn of extravagance and dissipation. The Greeks felt that if a woman showed a top bracelet which arched up into the palm, she would never bear children. Women with this sign often became vestal virgins and didn't marry.

4
Numerology

How can you read the facts about your character and destiny that are coded in your name? What is the power exerted on your life by your birth date? What is your lucky number and which are your lucky days?

Numerologists believe that all of us live under the influence of several numbers, the most important of which can be found by analysis of our name and date of birth. If these numbers, which guide our lives, are harmonious, our days will be happy and successful. If not, we will be in a constant state of inner conflict.

Since your birth date can't be altered, you may, if fate seems to be carrying you in the wrong direction, consider changing your name, the spelling of your name, or perhaps your middle initial, depending on the number whose influence you wish to adopt. Once you have done this, numerologists believe that the new number will take over and its vibrations will turn your life in a new direction. Today we talk about receiving "good vibrations" and "bad vibrations" from people and places, but numerologists have been discussing vibrations since the days of ancient Greece. Once you learn about numerology you may better un-

derstand why you are attracted to certain people whose numbers
—and vibrations—you will probably find to be harmonious with
your own.

The father of modern numerology is considered to be the
Greek philosopher Pythagoras, who lived in the sixth century B.C.
He taught that each number could be identified with certain
human attributes, affecting all matters to which it related. Pythagoras himself was named by the mysterious oracle at Delphi. Actually, the belief that a person's name contains, in some magical
fashion, the essence of his being and the promise of his destiny
goes back much further and is one of the oldest and most basic of
all mystical ideas. In many primitive tribes this conviction means
that if you wish death to an enemy you need only write his name
on a piece of stone or clay, recite the appropriate curses, and
bury it.

In our more civilized society we can see the influence of this
belief in the careful way in which parents select a name for their
child. If your mother and father gave you the name of a friend,
relative, or historical figure, it's probably not simply because they
like this particular name, but because they admire the person
who bears it. They are expressing a desire that you will grow up
with many of his fine qualities. They would, likewise, avoid calling you after someone whose example they disliked. Some parents call their sons Job, but most people wouldn't dare. Even
though biblical names are particularly popular today, it would
seem to be inviting bad luck to choose this one.

Once you become aware of our faith in the power of names
you will notice all sorts of examples. Orthodox Jews name a child
after a beloved ancestor as a commemoration. They believe that
if they were to break the law and name him after a living relative, that person might die. Catholics choose saints' names for

their children with considerable attention to the characteristics of their favorite holy man or woman. Changing names is closely associated with the idea of changing direction. People entering a new life course—in the church, in the field of entertainment, in the arts—often signal this step by adopting a new name. Name changing occurs all through the various books of the Bible, and Jesus, in selecting his apostles, picked new names for many of them to represent specific tasks and services he wished them to carry out.

Numerologists relate names to numbers by giving each letter a numerical equivalent so that names, in effect, *become* numbers. Number concepts and ideas about the power of numbers began before language. When early man looked about him for the meaning of the physical world and its relationship to his life, he saw what appeared to be an orderly universe based on laws which he could discover by careful observation of nature. The first mathematician was the man who looked at two rocks and then looked at two birds perched nearby and comprehended the relationship between them. From there he went on to notice other natural pairings: man and woman, day and night, earth and sky, birth and death. The concept of threeness in the natural world as well as in man's life came from such observations as sunrise-midday-sunset, man-woman-child, youth—middle age—old age. There are primitive tribes in which counting still includes only the concepts "one," "two," and "many." We count by tens because our ancestors calculated on the earliest adding machines, their fingers. In some primitive languages the word for "five" is the same as the word for "hand." The idea that certain numbers are "lucky" or "holy" appears in all religions and all societies, and it is a necessary part of the numerological belief that the laws of mathematics govern all life.

HOW TO FIND YOUR NAME NUMBER

To find out which numbers rule *your* life and how they relate to your personality, desires, and choice of career, begin at the beginning with the name your parents so carefully selected for you. Use your entire name as it appears on your birth certificate. If you are a girl you can see now why your life will change when you marry. Remember to pick a man whose name number is the same or vibrates in harmony with your own.

Each letter in a name has a particular number value:

$$
\begin{aligned}
A, \quad J, \text{ and } S &= 1 \\
B, \quad K, \text{ and } T &= 2 \\
C, \quad L, \text{ and } U &= 3 \\
D, \quad M, \text{ and } V &= 4 \\
E, \quad N, \text{ and } W &= 5 \\
F, \quad O, \text{ and } X &= 6 \\
G, \quad P, \text{ and } Y &= 7 \\
H, \quad Q, \text{ and } Z &= 8 \\
I \text{ and } R &= 9
\end{aligned}
$$

If this chart looks puzzling, check it against the next one. The numbers are assigned to letters just as they appear in sequence, but since numerology uses only single digits, they are numbered only up to nine. Compare the two charts and you'll see how the number-letter equivalents work. If you are going to try numerological fortune-telling on your friends at school, copy either chart on a card so that you will have a handy decoding reference.

A	B	C	D	E	F	G	H	I
1	2	3	4	5	6	7	8	9

J	K	L	M	N	O	P	Q	R
1	2	3	4	5	6	7	8	9

S	T	U	V	W	X	Y	Z
1	2	3	4	5	6	7	8

To see how name numbers are found, let's try a few samples.

ANGELA EVE THOMPSON

Check the chart for letter-number equivalents and separate the vowels from the consonants like this:

														Total
Vowels	1		5	1	5	5		6			6			= 29
	A	N	G	E	L	A	E	V	E	T	H	O	M P S O N
Consonants		5	7		3		4		2	8		4 7 1	5	= 46

The total of the vowels is 29, and since we only use single-digit numbers in numerology, we reduce 29 to one number by adding the digits:
$$2+9=11$$
Now do one further reduction:
$$1+1=2$$
The vowel number is 2.
The consonant number is 46 so we add:
$$4+6=10$$
$$1+0=1$$
The consonant number is 1.
Add the vowel number to the consonant number and you will find that Angela's name number is 3.
Here are a few more samples.

										Total
Vowels	6			6	5				=	17
	J O H N	R O B E R T S								
Consonants	1 8 5 9	2 9 2 1							=	37

The total of the vowels is 17.

$$1+7=8$$

The vowel number is 8.

The total of the consonants is 37.

$$3+7=10$$
$$1+0=1$$

The consonant number is 1.

Add the vowel number to the consonant number and you will find that John's name number is 9.

						Total
Vowels	3 1	9			=	13
	S U S A N	S M I T H				
Consonants	1 1 5 1 5	2 8			=	23

The total of the vowels is 13.

$$1+3=4$$

The total of the consonants is 23.

$$2+3=5$$

The consonant number is 5.

Add the vowel number to the consonant number.

Susan Smith has the same number as John Roberts!

					Total
Vowels	1	1 9	1	=	12
	M A R K	D A V I D	R Y A N		
Consonants	4 9 2	4 4 4	9 7 5	=	48

The total of the vowels is 12.

$$1+2=3$$

The vowel number is 3.

The total of the consonants is 48.

$$4+8=12$$

$$1+2=3$$

Mark's name number is 6.

Just remember to keep adding until all numbers are reduced to a single digit.

Once you have found your name number you can learn a good bit about why you are the sort of person who likes crowds or who likes to be alone, who paints well, who enjoys gourmet food, who is quick to anger, who loves children, who enjoys detailed work . . . who yearns to make money . . . who loves to travel . . . who can't sit still for very long. . . .

1

People whose name numbers equal the number one are coura-geous, inventive, and self-reliant. They are ambitious people who like to hold top positions. They really can be exciting people to know because of their original ideas and energy. This is the num-ber of the pioneer, the explorer, the inventor. Because number ones have considerable leadership ability, they often make good class officers and team captains. They have great powers of con-centration and drive which can be used for everyone's benefit.

But watch out. Every number contains qualities that we con-sider "good" and others that we consider negative or "bad." If someone you don't like has a name which equals this number, it's probably because he's boastful, conceited, and a real know-it-all.

When a number one *really* gets going on the wrong track he can be a tyrant and a bully. If you are a number one, remember that success will come if you use your ability to stand on your own feet without trying to dominate others.

2

The number two is a gentle and sensitive person who tends to be lovable and loving. Both number two girls and number two boys usually grow up to be warm and patient parents, kind friends, pleasant neighbors. They are born peace-makers, who want to live in harmony with their fellow man, resolve quarrels between enemies, act as go-betweens for others. Many twos are attracted to careers in diplomacy, for which they are marvelously suited. Interestingly, they tend to be music lovers, and they also are likely to be extremely tidy about their persons and possessions.

Unfortunately, these sensitive folk become extremely unhappy if they are criticized or feel that someone disapproves of something they've said or done. They often lack self-confidence and their shyness can be very painful to them socially. They are concerned about public opinion and maintaining a good reputation. They also tend to be physically timid and may never learn to enjoy sports that they consider dangerous. Sometimes a number two boy or girl will give you a real surprise. Because twos are so quiet and anxious to please, people think they can't be roused to anger. Watch out. Provoke a number two just a bit too much and you'll see that he can become extraordinarily hot-tempered.

If you are a two, always be aware of the fact that your mission in life is to be a troubleshooter, and your greatest satisfaction will come from playing this role well.

3

This is a many-sided person who is often extremely popular. With talents in many areas, a number three usually achieves easy success and inner happiness. He is imaginative, generous, and gay, with a fine sense of humor, which makes him the life of the party. He likes to do things on a big scale and enjoys luxury, good food, lavish entertainment. He takes himself less seriously than the number one, although he shares one's energy and inventiveness. Threes are ambitious people who often excel in positions of authority.

But sometimes threes dissipate their gifts and become superficial dilettantes, dabbling in many things and excelling in none. Their extravagance with money can lead them into serious trouble. It's not unusual to find a three who really has a lot of silly pride in his nature. Threes also tend to be jealous, so, despite their charm, they can be difficult friends.

Number three people are destined to help others recognize the power of optimism and cheer, so if you are a three, use these qualities well.

4

Number four is a neat, punctual, well-organized plugger. Just give a number four a difficult and tedious job and he'll dig right in. A four will excel in undertakings that require concentration, application, attention to detail. These are people who often have a high degree of mechanical ability, who like difficult word puzzles, who can figure out the endings of detective stories. A four is not an originator of new things or new ideas, but he brings the highest standards of excellence to carrying out someone else's plan. Fours are conscientious and practical. They are also thrifty; sometimes they go a bit further and become positively miserly.

Fours may be a bit too stern and lacking in humor. They often feel lonely and isolated because they don't make friends easily. They hate being hurried, as you may know if you are a four.

Fours are destined to play the role of organizer, bringing system and order to all projects they engage in.

5

Fives are restless talented people, who become wildly enthusiastic about a project but lose interest quickly and often leave things unfinished. They love change and new experiences, action, and excitement. They can be very persuasive and attractive and sometimes, like threes, they make excellent salesmen. Fives want to know a little about everything and everyone, and their curiosity can make them a bit too nosy at times. They adore travel, which never satisfies them. If you know someone who's always planning another trip, it's a good bet that he's a five.

Fives tend to be self-indulgent to a fault. If they aren't careful they can squander their money and their health in a life of excess and dissipation. When a five is really not a bit charming it's generally because his restlessness has made him totally unreliable as both a friend and a working partner. He will be a poor bet as a class officer, because he doesn't stick to jobs for long. He abhors routine and dullness and sometimes is unable to apply himself to the simplest necessary chore. When you hear an adult described as being youthful in the *wrong* sense—"He's never outgrown adolescence," is the way it's often put—he is probably a five who has misused his lively personality traits.

Your destiny, if you are a five, is to mix with all types of people and to play a role in current affairs.

6

Have you heard people described as being "The salt of the earth"? That's what a number six is like. This dependable, honest soul is cheerful and responsible. Sixes have strong humanitarian principles and enjoy both self-respect and the respect of others. Although they are as peace-loving as twos, they are much more ready to stand up and fight for what they believe in. Even as young children, sixes are passionately concerned with right and wrong, truth and fairness—for strangers as well as within their own family, school class, or neighborhood. As adults, they are excellent homemakers and talented gardeners, and active as workers and organizers in community action projects.

Sometimes a six, in his or her desire to protect loved ones, can be a bit overwhelming as a wife, husband, or parent. The six parent can be interfering and overanxious. A six child can seem pretty self-righteous and smug at times, but this is never due to pettiness. Sixes really are the sort of people most of us admire.

Are you a six? If so, your mission in life is to do good for less fortunate people than yourself.

7

Introspective artistic men and women who enjoy working alone will usually be found to be number sevens. They often are good writers, poets, or musicians, and they may become wealthy, although they have very little interest in pursuing material success for its own sake. They are not competitive at all. They are nature lovers who enjoy solitary walks, listening to music, deep contemplation. They can become totally preoccupied in the search for knowledge, and many sevens have a mystical tendency. They believe that knowledge is power, not money or position.

Life isn't easy for most sevens, who have a tendency to melancholy. They can be fault-finding and get on other people's nerves. They tend to consider frivolous many things other people enjoy and, particularly as children, may be considered by their contemporaries as rather strange, priggish, overly serious.

Sevens are destined to be educators, in the broadest sense, and knowledge is their road to happiness.

8

Eight is the number of material success and also of authority. Eights are capable of great deeds. They are energetic organizers, leaders who can command armies, voters, immense business empires. They give all to their undertakings and they often succeed brilliantly. They are busy, busy, busy people who love making money, taking part in a great many activities, working hard and playing hard. They are doers who rise early and love vigorous sports, "impossible" jobs.

You can understand that eights often go too far. They may become greedy for more and more money and power. Their strong ambition and demand for recognition can make them abusive and vengeful toward others. As husbands and wives they have so many consuming outside interests that they may be neglectful. As parents they may instill into their children too much love of material things. They may be careless of the feelings of others and feel superior to less dynamic people.

Don't play cards for money with an eight. They win every time.

Number eight boys and girls should keep in mind that their rewards will come from accomplishment, not from sheer financial gain.

9

Nines have the same talent for success as eights, but they turn more often to the arts and less to business, politics, and administration. They often achieve wealth, although they don't seek it with the purposefulness of the eight. They tend to be charitable and are often quite religious. Like fives they enjoy world travel and may often combine business and pleasure by finding jobs which entail travel to foreign lands.

Nines are very affectionate and will go to any extreme, sometimes to an unhappy conclusion, when trying to win the affection of someone they care for. They suffer in young adulthood from unrequited love, but most nines are able to make happy marriages as they become more mature. Despite their intensity and passion they tend to be fickle and they are very indiscreet. Don't tell a secret to a nine or you may soon find that everyone knows.

If you yourself are a nine remember to express love as service to others, not only toward one individual.

HOW TO FIND YOUR BIRTH NUMBER

Since numerologists believe that each person is sent into the world with a definite mission to accomplish, and since your birth date cannot be changed, it is most important in career planning to consider your birth number. The pleasure and value of doing the work for which you were intended is, after all, a major aspect of your life. If your birth date vibrates to an even number while your name vibrates to an odd number, a conflict has been set up between the logical and intuitive aspects of your nature, the practical and the spiritual. If your birth number is higher than your name number, troubles may overcome you because you are likely to be ruled by circumstances, but if the opposite is the case you are a person who can overcome difficulties and shape his life regardless of what misfortunes occur. If the two numbers are identical you are indeed fortunate, and you will enjoy harmony of spirit and ability which will lead to success in all your undertakings.

To find your birth number first translate the month of your birth into the calendar number it equals: January (1), February (2), March (3), April (4), May (5), June (6), July (7), August (8), September (9), October (10), November (11), December (12). Add this number to the day of the month on which you were born and add to this the four digits of the year of your birth.

July 9, 1958 = 7 / 9 / 1958:

$$
\begin{array}{r}
7 \\
9 \\
1 \\
9 \\
5 \\
\underline{8} \\
39
\end{array}
$$

$3 + 9 = 12$
$1 + 2 = 3$

If you were born on July 9, 1958, your birth number is: 3.

February 2, 1956 = 2 / 2 / 1956:

$$2$$
$$2$$
$$1$$
$$9$$
$$5$$
$$\underline{6}$$
$$25$$

$2 + 5 = 7$

If you were born on February 2, 1956, your birth number is: 7.

January 20, 1961 = 1 / 20 / 1961:

$$1$$
$$2$$
$$0$$
$$1$$
$$9$$
$$6$$
$$\underline{1}$$
$$20$$

$2 + 0 = 2$

If you were born on January 20, 1961, your birth number is: 2.

In planning a vocation, take into account the characteristics of the various numbers. Number seven is artistic. Numbers six and one don't require public recognition for happiness, and this might be helpful to a painter or poet. Scientific careers require the imagination of a one, three, or nine. Since eight is the number of financial success, an aspiring businessman should consider favorable a birth number of eight. If you wish to make a career in diplomacy, and your birth number and name number are both two, you have probably already been told that you're a natural.

Here are a few of the careers which are particularly suited to each birth number.

1. Pioneer, pilot, baker, typist, soldier, retailer, chef, explorer, executive, scientist.
2. Secretary, nurse, teacher, homemaker, editor, politician, diplomat, counsellor.
3. Salesman, disc jockey, politician, auctioneer, actor, entertainer, promoter, chemist.
4. Accountant, statistician, contractor, machinist, dentist, mathematician, typist.
5. Aviator, journalist, photographer, detective, travel writer, critic, salesman.
6. Doctor, research scientist, social worker, educator, florist, architect.
7. Writer, miner, farmer, researcher, homemaker, landscape gardener, designer, artist.
8. Banker, lawyer, executive, engineer, businessman, industrialist.
9. Missionary, nurse, doctor, minister, teacher, statesman, social worker.

HOW TO FIND YOUR LUCKY NUMBER

The day of your birthday—not the month or year—is your lucky number. If your birthday is March 8, for example, your lucky number is eight. Also favorable for you are all two- and three-digit numbers that can be reduced to eight, such as 17 (1 plus 7), 26 (2 plus 6), 224 (2 plus 2 plus 4), 485 (4 plus 8 plus 5=17, 1 plus 7=8). If the address of your house is either eight or one of these combinations, you will have particularly good luck while you live there.

Here is a calendar on which you can calculate the days of each month which are your lucky dates.

Any Month

date	1	2	3	4	5	6	7
lucky day for	1	2	3	4	5	6	7

date	8	9	10	11	12	13	14
lucky day for	8	9	1	2	3	4	5

date	15	16	17	18	19	20	21
lucky day for	6	7	8	9	1	2	3

date	22	23	24	25	26	27	28
lucky day for	4	5	6	7	8	9	1

date	29	30	31
lucky day for	2	3	4

If your birthday is March 8, your lucky days in each month are the 8th, the 17th, and the 26th. If your birthday is September 2, your lucky days each month are the 2nd, the 11th, the 20th, and the 29th. If your birthday is July 29, your lucky days are the same as those of the person born September 2—in other words, all the 2 days.

Each number also has a lucky day of the week:

The lucky day for a 1 birthday is Sunday

The lucky day for a 2 birthday is Monday

The lucky day for a 3 birthday is Thursday

The lucky day for a 4 birthday is Sunday

The lucky day for a 5 birthday is Wednesday

The lucky day for a 6 birthday is Friday

The lucky day for a 7 birthday is Monday

The lucky day for an 8 birthday is Saturday

The lucky day for a 9 birthday is Tuesday

Now, take the March 8 birthday. If one of the 8 days this month falls on a Saturday, that will be your luckiest day. If you have a 4 birthday, all 4 days are good, but the most favorable is one falling on a Sunday. If you are going to take a very decisive step in your life, plan to do it on this day. For everyone, certain days are particularly favorable for success in particular activities.

1 days (1, 10, 19, 28) are excellent for job hunting, starting a vacation, making new friends, looking for a new house.
2 days (2, 11, 29) are ideal days on which to forget yourself and think about others, visit the sick, write letters to distant friends and relatives.
3 days (3, 12, 21, 30) are days on which to give parties, and

they're also days on which to discuss differences with friends, because everyone feels most cheerful on 3 days.

4 days (4, 13, 22, 31) are days on which you should put your room in order, use up leftovers, do mending and repairs.

5 days (5, 14, 23) are days for adventure and freedom. Go on a long walk and take a sketchbook along, do something you've been wanting to try, take a long bike ride with no particular destination in mind.

6 days (6, 15, 24) are days on which you should talk things over with your parents and siblings, spend time reflecting about family differences if there have been recent problems.

7 days (7, 16, 25) are days for spiritual reflection, religious observance or reading of the Bible, listening to good music, contemplation of nature.

8 days (8, 17, 26) are days to attend to your finances, pay your bills, make a deposit in your savings account.

9 days (9, 18, 27) are days on which you should complete all jobs, duties, schoolwork, and other projects that you've left unfinished.

Numerology is filled with surprises. If you are named after your father you have probably developed a character much like his. If this is not so, remember—you don't have the same birth number, and that is the number which must have been more influential in forming your character. If you are a twin, you and your sibling share a birth number, but your names are different. Try finding the numbers for all members of your family—and let's hope they turn out to be compatible!

Something else you might try is finding the name and birth number of your favorite president, poet, actress, or baseball star.

You may acquire brand-new insights into the forces that shaped his or her career. And by the way—if your dog and cat keep up that quarreling, try giving them both new names that equal the number two, and see if this brings peace to the household.

5

Telling Fortunes
with Playing Cards

Two hundred years ago, when Josephine Tascher de la Pagerie was a young girl living on the Caribbean island of Martinique, a Creole fortune-teller with a well-worn pack of cards read her future. The totally unlikely prediction was that Josephine—the daughter of a sugar planter—would one day ascend the highest throne in Europe.

History does not tell us whether the card reader made such thrilling predictions often. It does affirm, however, that when this particular island girl was thirty-three years old and living in Paris, the widow of a man who had been sent to the guillotine, she met and married Napoleon Bonaparte and became empress of France.

The origins of fortune-telling with cards are somewhat obscure. We know that cards were in existence in several European countries in the fourteenth century. Some experts say that the Romany gypsies, who arrived in Italy from Arabia and Egypt during this period, first introduced cards to Europe. Others claim that they were brought from the East by crusaders returning with these and other mementoes of their travels. They are

Playing cards take many forms. Here are a few unusual examples from China (above), India (center), and Persia (below).

thought by some historians to have been invented much earlier in China. There is little argument about the fact that cards were first used only for divination, and that the idea of using cards in games and gambling followed soon after their appearance in Europe.

The idea of four suits seems to be basic to even the earliest cards, despite differences in the sizes of the early cards, their design, and the number of cards in a deck.

The playing-card suits as we know them today first developed in France in the early fifteenth century. The British adopted the

French symbols for the suits and renamed them. They also designed the picture cards or court cards, and ours today are still costumed in the manner of the court of Henry VII. The Germans, Spanish, and Italians developed their own suit terms, and in some instances changed the symbols. Old German cards use the symbols heart, leaf, bell, and acorn.

Card playing has been popular virtually all over the world up through the centuries, and reading with cards has remained a favorite fortune-telling technique. It is not an easy skill to master, because it depends a good bit on individual interpretation. The cards each tell a snatch of the story. The card reader must learn to fill in the details.

WHAT THE CARDS TELL

Any gypsy will tell you that when telling fortunes with the standard fifty-two-card deck of playing cards you must discard from the deck all cards with numbers below seven, leaving a deck composed of four sevens, four eights, four nines, four tens, four jacks, four queens, four kings, and four aces, or thirty-two cards in all.

Plan to keep a special deck of cards which you use for fortune-telling purposes only. Picture cards used to be designed with one head, but since the turn of the century double-headed cards have been standard. Since in some instances it is important to know whether a card falls in reverse position, you should prepare your deck by marking one end of each card, which will then become the top. Use a felt pen of some bright color other than red—green and blue show up best—and make a large dot or check or x or some other sign so that you can instantly spot a reversed card in a group laid out on the table to be read.

In the instructions to follow, the term "reader" refers to you

The year is 1901 and this elegantly dressed woman is having her fortune told by an exotic card reader.

and the term "questioner" refers to the person whose fortune you are telling. Most methods of divination by cards require that the questioner decide at the beginning on a card to represent him or her which will be known as the "questioner's card." This must be selected by traditional rules. The card must be either a king or queen, matching the questioner's sex, and must further be keyed to his or her general hair and skin coloring. Someone who is really fair—a blue-eyed blonde with pale skin—must pick the king or queen of diamonds. People who are a bit darker should pick hearts. Clubs come next, for an average brunette, and the king or queen of spades is used to represent someone who is extremely dark-skinned and dark-haired. Do not remove this card from the deck.

To perform a reading, sit across the table from the questioner. Reader and questioner should approach each other in a serious manner. Select a quiet room in which no one else is present.

There are innumerable methods, known as "spreads," for laying out the cards, many of them very ancient. To begin, both reader and questioner must handle the deck, imparting and mingling their vibrations and sensitizing the cards. Regardless of the type of reading, the questioner will be the one to cut and shuffle the cards. Instruct him to cut using his left hand only, lifting part of the deck and placing it to the left and then taking the right-hand pile and placing it on top of the other—never the reverse. Four different spreads are described on pages 116 through 120.

Regardless of how you spread the cards, the card meanings will remain the same. The charts which follow give the significance of each card in your thirty-two-card fortune-telling deck. These meanings, however, are simply hints and suggestions, capable of various interpretations depending on the insights of the reader and the combination of cards presented. It is really of enormous value in card reading to have enough intuition or ESP to fill in the gaps, read the cards skillfully, and weave a tale that suits the questioner. At first you may simply find yourself relaying a series of disjointed facts, but you must practice relating the possible suggested meanings of the cards into character analyses and predictions which are coherent, plausible, and interesting.

SOME METHODS OF LAYING OUT CARDS

1. After the questioner has cut, shuffled, and recut the deck, the reader may spread them—with a quick and graceful motion—into a fan. This takes practice, so if you knock them all over the floor just pick them up with dignity and try again. The faces of the cards will be down. Ask the questioner to select thirteen cards. Then stack these cards carefully, face up, and spread them into a horseshoe shape facing you. Put the others aside. If the card that has been decided on as the questioner's card appears, the spread is considered lucky and the most favorable interpretation must be put on all the cards. Look first for combinations and read them. Then proceed from left to right, making whatever associations you can between cards that lie next to each other.

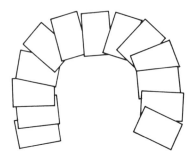

2. Here is another way to read fortunes with cards. Have the questioner cut, shuffle, and recut the cards with his left hand.

The reader then spreads them, face down, into a fan, and the questioner picks nine cards from the deck. Put the others aside. The reader takes the nine cards and lays them out on the table in a diamond shape like this.

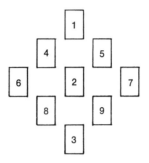

The numbers indicate the order in which they are put down. The card numbered as one will be the most important, indicating, if it is a heart, success in love; if it is a club, success in school and good health; if a diamond, financial success; if a spade, trouble and disappointment. Cards two and three indicate the amount of time that will pass before certain events which will be predicted come to pass, and this depends simply on their number value—if high, a long time; if low, a short time. Picture cards indicate a long delay. Read cards four and five together, checking the meanings, to see whether the person's good fortune is likely to increase or decrease. Cards six and seven will refer to love and marriage, and you must interpret their meanings accordingly. If the questioner's card appears near a picture card of the opposite sex this indicates a very happy marriage. Cards eight and nine deal with the immediate future. For instance, if these happen to be the ace of hearts and the king of diamonds, it might mean that the questioner is about to go to a party where she will meet a boy who could bring problems into her life. She should be warned of this chance.

3. A simple bit of card play will answer the question, "Will my wish be granted?" The questioner does not reveal his wish but simply asks the question aloud. The questioner then cuts the cards and checks the cut card—the bottom one of the right-hand pack—and shows it to the reader. Then he shuffles and reshuffles the cards and cuts the pack again, approximately in half. The reader takes the deck and deals it out into three piles. She then turns the cards over face up and spreads each pile downward and examines them.

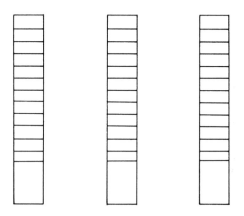

If the questioner's card and the cut card appear in the same pile, the wish will certainly be granted. The number of cards falling between these two indicates the amount of time this will take, and you must use your ESP to decide whether it refers to days, weeks, months, or years. If the two cards are not in the same pack the outcome is uncertain. If the nine of spades, the card of great disappointment, is in the same pack as the cut card, the answer is definitely no, and if this card lies between the cut card and questioner's card when they are in the same pile, the wish will be granted but it will turn out to have been a bad wish to begin with and will result in misfortune. Look for other clues. If the nine of hearts, indicating success and joy in a coming venture, appears near either the cut card or the questioner's card, the prospects are excellent that the wish will indeed come true.

4. One way of reading fortunes with cards involves dealing by threes. First select the questioner's card. After the cards have been cut, shuffled, and recut, start dealing off the top, taking three at a time and turning them over, face up and side by side, for examination. If two or three cards of the same suit appear in one group of three, take the highest one and place it in the center of the table. Return others to the deck unless three cards with the same number or picture appear at once. In this case take all three and place them side by side in the center of the table. Reshuffle the remaining cards and repeat dealing by threes, selecting cards for the center of the table by the same method until twelve or sixteen cards are on the table, one of which must be the questioner's card. If it has appeared by the time twelve cards are out, stop there. If it has not appeared by the time you have sixteen cards out, start again. Place the cards, in the order in which you withdrew them, in a circular arrangement.

Put the rest of the deck aside.

First interpret the matching cards.

Next count seven clockwise from the questioner's card and interpret this card.

Continue reading each seventh card until you have finished all the cards.

Next, pick up the cards, shuffle them, and deal them out into four piles. Have the questioner select one pile. These cards contain the news of his immediate future. Lay out the three or four cards and read them together. Look for the relationships among their meanings that will help you to turn them into a final prediction.

MEANING OF THE CARDS

HEARTS ♥

Hearts are the symbols of romance and marriage, of good friends and loving homes. They signify festive occasions and hospitality.

seven: You will receive news from someone dear to you. This is also the card of happy marriage and of tranquility, of wisdom and reflection.

eight: You will form a friendship with a pretty fair-skinned girl of very pleasant disposition.

nine: This card indicates success and joy in some coming venture. There is a suggestion here of trophies, of victory, of winning a game or contest.

ten: Happiness and love are signified by this card. This person may also have many children or be a member of a large family.

jack: A young unmarried man, who may be a suitor, is signified. He is a pleasure-lover and an enthusiastic traveler. He is also an excellent host.

queen: A light-haired amiable woman, very friendly and helpful. She is a dear relative or a close friend.

king: A generous fair-haired man will affect your life. He is a man of stature, active in public life, highly esteemed by others.

ace: Some pleasant news, which may be a party invitation, is coming to you. This card also indicates feasting and celebrations.

DIAMONDS ♦

Diamonds symbolize money and money-making ventures, worldly possessions in general, business matters, travel, and sometimes unexpected events.

seven: This is certain to mean a present is coming. It also signifies good news in general.

eight: This card indicates a visit which may be to the country or be from someone who lives on a farm or in a rural area.

nine: Some new type of start in school or work is indicated, but it may result from quarrels at home or on the job, or from difficulties at school.

ten: A trip, perhaps a change of residence, is signified by this card. It may include a sea voyage or residence of a temporary nature near a body of water.

jack: A pleasant young stranger, possibly in uniform, is coming. Watch for him. He is a good person who will bring you luck.

queen: A light-haired woman is indicated. She is not necessarily friendly and she may be someone from another state or country. Something scandalous may happen.

king: A blonde boy or man, or possibly a redhead, with a rosy complexion and a sharp temper, is signified by this card. There may be trouble with him. Watch out.

ace: This card refers to business letters or literary works. In some instances it may be a lawsuit. Whatever it is, it's important to you.

CLUBS ♣

Clubs are the leading suit, symbolizing happiness, good news, success in school, and social popularity. They are also associated with printed matter, particularly letters and legal documents.

seven: Money is coming to you, either in cash, fortunate investments which will increase in value, or the repayment of a debt. This card has a secondary meaning which is that a dark child is affecting your life.

eight: A dark-haired girl or woman will fall in love with you. If questioner is a girl this person will, instead, be a deeply devoted friend. This person is very extravagant with money, so be careful.

nine: Unexpected wealth is in your future, probably coming to you through a will. It is also possible that you will receive it as a gift or by marrying a wealthy person.

ten: This card also signifies great wealth. With it will come esteem, possibly even fame. Something noteworthy you have done will bring you this income.

jack: The jack of clubs signifies a dark man of romantic nature who will come into your life. He may be a lover or he may be a very warm friend. He is a studious and home-loving person.

queen: This card also indicates a dark girl or woman. She will be a very close friend for a long time, or is already. In personality she is frank, talkative, and honest.

king: A dark young man who is or will be a true friend is signified. He will become a good husband and an upstanding citizen as he matures. He is scholarly, perhaps a teacher.

ace: This card brings sensational news and great prosperity.

It is the most important card, signifying financial success, success in schoolwork, and excellent health.

SPADES ♠

Spades symbolize misfortune, worry, sickness, lack of money, and a great number of life's serious disappointments.

seven: This card warns of the death of a friend or a very unhappy anxious period of time which might result from the serious but not fatal illness of a close friend.

eight: This card indicates illness of mind or body, possibly due to an injury. It also indicates rest from work and a period of quiet and inaction.

nine: A very unfortunate card, this indicates sorrow and is, by many gypsies, considered the most unfortunate card in the deck. It predicts defeat, breakup of families, failure in general.

ten: This may indicate a prison sentence or worrisome matters which begin with the arrival of a letter of some sort. It also indicates jealousy.

jack: A dark man who acts as a messenger is symbolized by this card. He may bring you unwelcome news. This card is an evil omen to lovers, signifying problems from an outsider or betrayal.

queen: A dark woman, possibly a widow or divorcee, is indicated. She may be a false friend.

king: A dark ambitious man, who may be a lawyer or other representative of the law, or possibly a doctor. He should be feared.

ace: This card also indicates legal matters and difficulties. It also suggests abandonment and suffering.

On the simplest level, if a young woman is the questioner and jacks keep appearing, you can be sure she has many suitors. If one of them appears with the nine of spades, she may be about to make a serious error in selecting one to marry. Or let's say you turn up a ten of diamonds, signifying a trip, in association with a king of hearts, signifying a generous fair-haired man who has the esteem of others. If the questioner is an eighth-grader it is unlikely that the fair-haired man is her husband. If this card appears associated with a card indicating travel it may be her brother, but that too is not as likely as interpretation as this one: her father, who is a man with light coloring and who is a distinguished and important person in the community, is going to take the family on a trip sometime in the coming month—a trip which probably will be to the beach or to a lake. If the questioner is blonde her parents may be also. If summer vacation is near, this is a particularly likely interpretation. If the questioner is an older woman the fair-haired man is probably her husband. If you know the woman and she is widowed or divorced, it may be her son, or then again it is more likely to be a man of her age—someone she is about to meet on a vacation.

Here is another example. Let's say you turn up a nine of hearts along with the eight of spades. Check the following charts for the card meanings. This would appear to indicate a conflict: a victory along with illness or accident. The likely interpretation would be that the person is about to win an award for some athletic feat, but that soon afterward he will injure himself in a game or contest and have to endure a period of quiet and recovery. Or perhaps the victory itself will be won in a struggle against illness.

Here is one more case. Let us say you have turned up a queen of hearts along with the nine of clubs. It is possible that your delightful aunt is going to bring you a present. It is also possible that she will die and you will inherit her money. There are many other ways of interpreting this combination. The reader must decide which is the most likely interpretation, and this is essentially what the art of fortune-telling is all about.

Begin by studying the meanings of the four suits. All cards relate in some way to the general significance of the entire suit. You can probably memorize the meanings of the picture cards rather easily, and you might consider, if you don't want to have to check the book constantly, noting down some of the meanings on small cards which you can consult less conspicuously. If you want to be a real gypsy card reader, you must get to know the card meanings well enough so that you don't have to refer to any written material.

Be careful not to give too dire a reading, even when your spread is littered with spades. Life's difficulties can often be overcome, and if you are shocked to find that things really look dreadful for your questioner, you might tell her that life is going to present her with many problems and she must work to acquire the strength which will help her to meet them.

Remember always that the card meanings in the chart *suggest* —they do not *tell* what is in store. You are the one who must discover their meaning in relation to what you know or sense about the character and circumstances of the questioner.

Reverse meanings: In general, if a card falls in a reverse position in fortune-telling, the meaning is reversed or the prediction is in danger of not coming true—unless the news is already bad, in which case it becomes worse! When the questioner's card comes out reversed it indicates that he or she is in an anxious and disturbed state of mind at the time.

Certain significant combinations should be remembered. Two aces falling side by side indicate that the questioner will marry soon or is already married. Three aces are an excellent sign of success, and four a certain one. If any or all of the aces are reversed, all one's current success in love, school, and business is in danger.

Four kings are extraordinarily lucky, indicating honors of every sort. Three and two indicate luck as well, but not on so large a scale.

Two queens falling together indicate a happy meeting between friends, and four queens a very important party.

Four jacks, like four queens, indicate popularity, friendly partying, and good times. Three jacks may be a warning of unfaithfulness in a friend, and two of an argument.

Two tens falling together indicate a change of school, job, or residence. Four tens indicate that such a change will be very successful, although three tens hint at improper conduct and possibly some dishonesty.

Two, three, or four nines indicate good news is coming soon which will be a great surprise.

Eights falling together are not so fortunate, showing that difficulties are near. What you desire most is not attainable at this time. However, two red eights falling together are a sign that the questioner is about to have a new wardrobe.

Sevens falling together warn of disputes and possible scandal. Beware of an enemy who wishes you harm.

Once you have learned to read playing cards you might like to try the more difficult technique of reading tarot cards, described in the next chapter.

6

The Mysterious Tarot Cards

In 1392 the royal treasurer to the king of France, Charles VI, entered a payment in his books to an astrologer and mystic named Jacquemin Grigonneur, who had fashioned three games of cards for the amusement of the king. The king was, at this time, suffering from a mysterious form of mental derangement, and it appears that Grigonneur had latched on to the modern idea that this diversion might serve as a form of recreational therapy. Seventeen of these tarot (TAR-ō) cards are preserved today in the National Library in Paris.

In the previous chapter we learned that the earliest cards of which we have record date from the fourteenth century. At this time all cards were of a type known as "tarots," as distinguished from the playing cards of today, which were invented a century later.

Tarots were primarily used for divination, but a game named tarocchi, which is played with a tarot deck, originated in Italy in the late Middle Ages and is still popular in Central Europe.

The tarot pack is larger than a deck of playing cards. There are seventy-eight cards, rather than fifty-two, and the cards

This set of tarot cards dates from the sixteenth century.

themselves are bigger. Fifty-six of these cards compose what is known as the Lesser Arcana, and they are divided into four suits of fourteen cards each. The suits are known as Cups, Batons or Wands, Swords, and Coins or Pentacles. Each suit has number cards from one through ten plus four picture cards: King, Queen, Knight, and Jack (or Page). The other twenty-two cards form the Greater Arcana. They are symbolic picture cards, each with a name and a number shown in Roman numerals. Often, but not always, the French name is used on the Greater Arcana cards.

Today's tarot cards are based on a set which were made by a hairdresser named Etteilla, who lived at the time of the French Revolution. Etteilla adapted the ancient tarots, which varied in number and design, to his own standardized system, and assigned the French names to the Greater Arcana. The result is what we now regard as the authentic tarot deck. (Actually, this man's name was Alliette, and he reversed the spelling in assign-

Examples of cards from three different tarot decks in use today.

ing his name to the cards for reasons that history does not record.)

Tarot cards are extremely mysterious at best, and it is recommended that you obey all the rules about their care and handling. Do not let other people handle your tarots, and never use them for games. Experts advise that you keep them wrapped in purple silk or velvet, since the color purple is believed to absorb vibrations. This is so that when you take them out they will be cleansed of all previous vibrations and associations from other readings. When you buy your pack of tarots you might consider sleeping with them under your pillow for three nights, the time deemed necessary for the cards to pick up your personal magnetism. During a reading, you and your subject must both handle the cards to mingle your vibrations, as is the case in telling fortunes with playing cards.

READING TAROTS

No one knows precisely how the earliest tarot cards were spread for interpretation. In recent centuries both the symbols on the cards and the manner of spreading the tarots for reading have changed. Each reader should, through practice, give his own interpretations to the cards, with the following meanings given as general clues, trends, and indications, influences in life which can be radically altered. You may also, as with playing cards, evolve your own method for spreading the cards. The elaborate pictures, as well as the suggestive and mysterious names on each card, are intended to stimulate the intuition and imagination of the reader. He then selects the meaning which seems to relate best to the questioner, the other cards on the table—particularly those to either side—and the specific advice the questioner may be seeking.

Since there are seventy-eight cards in a complete tarot deck and since the use of the entire deck becomes extremely intricate, we will deal only with the twenty-two cards of the Greater Arcana. On the following pages you will find these cards described by number, French title, English translation, traditional picture (which may or may not be the one used on your cards), most common meaning, and reverse meaning. If you accomplish the difficult job of learning to read fortunes using the twenty-two Greater Arcana cards only and you wish to learn more, look in libraries and bookshops for one of the several fine books which are devoted entirely to this detailed and difficult subject.

The beginner should remove the twenty-two Greater Arcana cards from the deck and seat himself opposite the questioner at a table. Mondays and Fridays are considered particularly favorable days for reading tarot cards unless the weather is stormy. Wind, heavy rain, lightning, and thunder are believed to interfere with the magnetism and vibrations involved in reading the cards.

As reader you should place the twenty-two cards in sequence by numbers with the unnumbered Fool placed either at the beginning, in the middle, at the end, or between the twentieth and twenty-first card. The questioner must be asked to shuffle the cards and place them in a pack face down in front of the reader. The cards, which are single-faced, unlike playing cards, are always read facing the reader. As is the case with playing cards, the meanings remain the same, regardless of which spread is used.

SPREADING THE TAROTS: TWO METHODS

1. Here is one method for spreading and reading the Major Arcana cards. The reader takes the cards and, starting from the top of the deck, turns them over one at a time from left to right,

placing them in the manner shown below. Any card which falls facing the questioner is considered reversed, and the reversed meaning is to be assigned to this card.

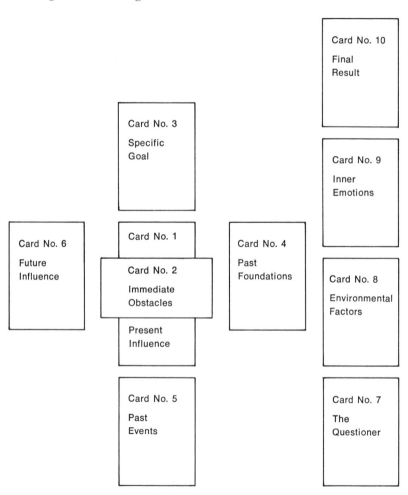

Now concentrate and read the cards.

Card number 1 will tell you what sort of atmosphere the questioner lives in at this time.

Card number 2 will indicate the problems which lie ahead in the near future.

Card number 3 will show what the questioner can hope to accomplish in his current situation.

Card number 4 will tell you about the questioner's past and how he attacks his problems.

Card number 5 tells about the influence of events which have just occurred or are occurring at this time.

Card number 6 shows what will influence the questioner in the very near future.

Card number 7 tells the present attitude of the questioner in relation to the position he now finds himself in.

Card number 8 relates to the questioner's position in his family, his school, his occupation. It tells about his influence on the people around him.

Card number 9 reveals inner hopes and fears and may also tell about how these will change in the questioner's mind as he grows older.

Card number 10 indicates the result that will come from the varying circumstances and personality traits revealed in the preceding nine cards. It hints at the future in the broadest possible sense.

2. Here is a method for giving advice on a particular problem. Ask the questioner to state his or her question. It might be something like this: "Will I succeed in getting a role in the school play?" or "Will my disagreement with my parents be resolved?" or "Am I suited for a career as a scientist?"

The reader then asks the questioner to cut the cards in the usual fashion and deals out the following spread:

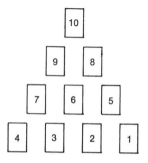

In this case, the cards are dealt face down, and then each card is turned over, from left to right. The reader views each separately and then the whole.

The first four cards represent the questioner's past. Check their suggested meanings and see what you can learn.

The next row of three cards represents the questioner's present.

The next row of two cards represents the questioner's immediate future.

The tenth card represents the final answer to the question, which takes into account all that has been revealed in the other nine cards. You will have to concentrate very carefully on each row of cards—and how you have interpreted them—and relate it to the next row, and *its* meaning.

Reading tarots well requires of the practitioner a mature sense of responsibility. Some questioners may come to you in a very troubled state of mind. If you predict disaster, death, destruction, abandonment, this is unfair and cruel, even if certain unfortunate cards keep turning up. Tarot does not deal with fate, but with trends and possibilities, which can always be changed. Unfortunate cards indicate a warning that problems may be approaching that can usually be overcome with courage and determination and application to work. They may also indicate troubles in the *past* that have already been overcome and have left the subject stronger.

Weave your observations and intuitions into a story, as you did in reading fortunes with playing cards. Practice is essential, and as you become more and more familiar with your cards and their meanings you will develop a personal style and increased fluency in this very difficult art.

MEANINGS OF THE TAROT CARDS: GREATER ARCANA

O The Fool—Le Mat: A young man, traditionally in jester's clothing. This card signifies that a choice is being offered and the person must avoid folly, excess, extravagance, frivolity. Reverse meaning: He will choose the wrong road through thoughtlessness.

I The Magician or Juggler—Le Bateleur: A magician stands behind a table bearing a number of symbolic objects. He holds a wand in his left hand. This card symbolizes originality and skill, willpower and mastery, the ability to choose one's own action and to complete what one starts. Reverse meaning: lack of all these capabilities and willpower used toward destructive ends.

II The High Priestess—Junon: A goddess wearing a headdress She is a strong, broad-shouldered woman. This card indicates serenity and wisdom, learning and understanding. It also stands for the mysterious future. If the inquirer is male, this card is a female presently in his life or soon to appear. Reverse meaning: ignorance, shallowness, conceit, ruthlessness.

III The Empress—L'Impératrice: A woman wearing a long gown and a crown. The Empress signifies fertility, marriage, sound understanding of people and their problems, action, and attainment. Reverse meaning: indecision, inaction, delay, and anxiety.

IV The Emperor—L'Empereur: A regal-looking aging man with a beard and drooping mustache sits on a throne. He wears a crown and carries a scepter. This card symbolizes worldly power, ambition, high intellect, leadership, and the realization of goals. Reverse meaning: weakness, lack of ability, immaturity, fear of authority.

V The Heirophant or Pope—Jupiter: An elderly man wearing a crown and holding a scepter. The meaning of this card is mercy and kindness, goodness, forgiveness, and also conformity. Reverse meaning: unwise excess of generosity, gullibility, renunciation of religion, openness to unconventional ideas.

VI The Lovers—L'Amoureux: Tarot cards show here a young man and a young woman. In some cases a serpent in the picture suggests the Adam and Eve scene; in others, an evil-looking man stands by to represent vice. The card symbolizes beauty, harmony, and attraction. It suggests a test or a trial, temptation, the struggle between love of man and love of God. Reverse meaning: failure when tested, infidelity in marriage, loss of love and divorce, inability to overcome a deep personal problem.

VII The Chariot—Le Chariot: A fair young king or conqueror dressed in armor, with a chariot. The card indicates war and vengeance, trouble and adversity, greatness, victory, conquest, and triumph over financial problems, health problems, enemies. Reverse meaning: Inability to meet responsibility and face reality, possibly an unrighteous victory.

VIII Justice—La Justice: This is a crowned female figure holding scales of judgment in one hand and a double-edged sword in the other. This card signifies justice, balance, fairness, and honor. It indicates legal matters with a good outcome and satisfaction in accomplishments. Reverse meaning: unfairness, intolerance, violence, injustice, and false accusations.

IX The Hermit—L'Ermite: A bearded old man dressed like a monk carries a lantern. This card represents prudence, caution, care. It indicates a possible journey. It also means thrift and self-denial. Reverse meaning: hastiness, immaturity, impatience, unreasonable caution, ignorance.

X The Wheel of Fortune—La Roue de Fortune: The wheel is shown revolving on its axis with various symbolic figures. This card indicates fortune, luck, and destiny, the ups and downs of life, success in your chosen career, unexpected opportunity. Reverse meaning: failure, ill fortune, bad luck, success followed by a fall.

XI Strength—La Force: Some cards show a warrior; others show either Hercules or a woman struggling with a lion and subduing it. This is the card of energy, courage, and determination. It signifies spiritual strength as well as physical strength. A man finding this card in his spread will have a woman in his life with these qualities, and a woman whose spread shows this card will have the strength to overcome difficulties through patience. Reverse meaning: weakness, pettiness, abuse of power, physical illness.

XII The Hanged Man—Le Pendu: A man is hanging upside

down, suspended by one foot. His hands are behind his back. This card signifies surrender and sacrifice, particularly *self*-sacrifice. It indicates the efforts which may be required to reach a desired goal, but may also mean losses, reverses, and abandonment. Reverse meaning: unwillingness to make the effort required, selfishness, vanity.

XIII Death—La Mort: A skeleton is either riding a horse or using a scythe on bare earth. He suggests the inability to change the past. The card signifies sudden change, loss, failure, destruction, death. Death may not be physical, but may mean death of a former way of life and a rebirth into new experiences, a new era. Reverse meaning: immobility, recovery from a serious illness or accident, inertia, stagnation.

XIV Temperance—Tempérance: A picture of an angel with wings symbolizes temperance. In some, the angel pours liquid from one vessel into another, symbolizing the flowing of the past into the present and into the future. This card suggests moderation, patience, thrift, friendship, good management, discipline, and a balanced life. Reverse meaning: discord, impatience, unhappy marriage, arguments, and fighting.

XV The Devil—Le Diable: The devil is often shown naked with cloven hooves and a pitchfork. His head is horned. The card indicates disaster and violence, enslavement, shock, ravage, downfall, lack of principle, and a relentless drive for power and wealth. Reverse meaning: freedom from bondage, weakness and timidity, the beginning of spiritual understanding.

XVI The House of God, also called The Tower—La Maison de Dieu: A tower is being struck by lightning and usually two human figures are shown falling to the ground. Having been struck, the tower is now the devil's tower. The card signifies disruption and calamity, sudden unhappy events, breakdown and undoing, and dreadful danger, which may be physical, spiritual, or financial. Reverse meaning: continued disaster, but to a lesser degree. It may involve false accusations, oppression, inability to change.

XVII The Star—L'Étoile: Traditionally, a young woman kneels by a pool of water, pouring water from a beaker into the lake, signifying new ideas. The meaning of this card is hope and trust, a bright future, and a person who will come into the inquirer's life and have a very strong effect on it. Good health and influence over others are also indicated. Reverse meaning: hope unfulfilled, pessimism, bad luck, physical and mental illness.

XVIII The Moon—La Lune: This may show a man playing a lute for a woman on a balcony with a large moon overhead, or a dog and a wolf barking at the moon, shown in profile. The card implies trickery and deception, dishonesty, disgrace, and dishonor due to insincere friends. This card means danger. Reverse meaning: minor deceptions and unimportant mistakes. Peace of mind will be regained at some cost.

XIX The Sun—Le Soleil: A great sun with human face shines down, generally on a young boy and girl who either dance or sit on the ground holding a book of knowledge. This is the card of satisfaction and successful achievement, of well-being and friendship, unselfish love and happy marriage, pleasure, good health, and happy reunions. Reverse meaning: unhappiness or a lesser degree of satisfaction, a broken engagement, loss of a valued object.

XX Judgment—Le Jugement: An angel with wings rides on a

cloud and blows a trumpet. This is the card of rebirth, readjustment, new beginning, change of position, promotion. Reverse meaning: separation and loss of money, physical frailty, inability to achieve happiness, delay and postponement of necessary action.

XXI The World—Le Monde: A woman stands within a wreath, while a lion and a bull, guardians of truth, stand below. This card represents success and perfection. It indicates triumph in all undertakings and the esteem of friends and others. Reverse meaning: inability to complete a job, a lack of imagination, poor powers of concentration.

7

Tea Leaf Reading

Americans today have become so accustomed to the use of tea bags—and the idea that tea leaves must at any cost be kept *out* of the cup—that tea leaf reading is not nearly so popular as it used to be. In England, however, where brewing a proper pot of tea is a way of life, looking for suggestive shapes formed by the leaves in the bottom of the cup is a common pastime. Although reading tea leaves is a gypsy skill, many an English housewife, sitting in the kitchen sipping with a neighbor, is irresistibly tempted to peer into her friend's future when her cup is empty.

Reading tea leaves is fun, and if you really can't cope with loose tea, it's pretty easy to cheat. If you've used a tea bag, simply cut it open with a scissors. This suggestion is given, of course, as an emergency measure. If you brew tea correctly from the start, it will taste better, and the fortune is more likely to come true.

Give the pot a stir before pouring the tea so the leaves won't stay at the bottom. Use a cup which is broad and shallow, not tall and steep. A white cup is best for seeing the pattern of the leaves clearly. Drink up, and when there is only about a teaspoon of liquid left in the bottom of your friend's cup and a nice pile of leaves, instruct her to take the cup in her left hand and swirl it three times toward her heart, in a counterclockwise direction. She should turn it vigorously, causing the leaves to rise up along the sides of the cup. When this has been done she should be instructed to place the cup upside down in the saucer.

After the cup has had a few seconds to drain, the reader turns it upright and begins to examine the patterns formed by the leaves along its bottom and sides. Reading tea leaves is really a challenge to the imagination, because the shapes identified as people, animals, and all sorts of other objects really look most of all like a lot of wet tea. Squint a bit and take your time. If you can spot three leaves in a row or a long thin trail of leaves, that means a journey. If you see something that looks even slightly like a snake crossing this line or sitting around nearby, you might tell the client that she is going to take a journey, but she must beware of dangers on this trip. A snake *always* means danger. Initials can often be spotted and so can numbers. These may be of some importance in the questioner's life. The initial might be that of a loved one or an enemy. A number can mean whatever seems right to you at the time, depending on what other signs can be located in the cup.

Animal shapes are often seen. The image of a dog indicates a faithful friend, whereas a cat suggests a false friend who will betray. A mouse or rat (any small blob with a tail) means money troubles. A horse's head, on the other hand, indicates a lover. Birds near the cup's handle tell of good news coming soon.

The handle of the cup stands for the person's home, and leaves near the handle refer to things happening at home rather than at work or school. Leaves near the rim indicate present events, and those at the bottom of the cup, more distant happenings. Circles tell of a job completed, and wavy lines show that everything's up in the air.

Here are some other commonly seen shapes and their meanings. Try to connect one shape with another so that a story emerges. Be serious, look carefully, speak in a voice filled with mystery. Magic words, if you know some, can be muttered while you peer into the cup. Tea leaf reading requires the same skill used in telling fortunes with cards. Relate the meanings into a

Try reading these tea leaves for practice.

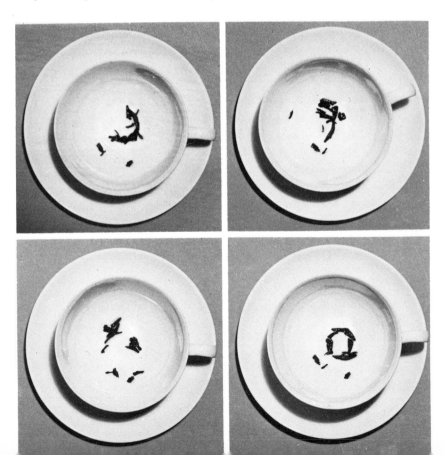

chain of connected predictions. Don't simply make a series of unconnected statements.

Airplane—Advance in life due to personal effort.
Mountains—Ambitions will be realized, but not without effort.
Ants—Perseverance and thrift will stand you in good stead.
Man—A visitor is arriving.
Ship—This is always a symbol of good fortune.
Wings—Good or bad messages are coming, you decide. "Wings" may look like "birds," which are definitely good news.
Table—A sign of reunion of family or old friends.
Star—Sudden dangers, accidents, and catastrophic happenings.
Flower—This refers to the joys of youth.
Clock—Recovery from a severe illness.
Butterfly—Beware of too much frivolity and gaiety.
Cake—A wedding is indicated.
Bow—This is a symbol of good luck.
Egg—Successful changes, new projects.
Face—Seeing a face in the bottom of the cup indicates that the person will make a discovery.
Fish—This is a very fortunate symbol, indicating success in money matters.
Hand—This is a symbol which means friendship and good works and the assistance of others.
Hat—A new occupation or marriage is indicated.
Leaf—News, messages, love letters.
Necklace—Many admirers.
House—A happy and prosperous life. This is also a symbol of safety and independence.
Moon—A quarter moon is a sign of new undertakings. A full moon is a sign of romance.

Clouds—You are about to pass through a period of trouble.

Ring—Predicts marriage if found near the top of the cup. If clouds are nearby, this may be unwise.

Pot—This is a sign of service to others, at which you excel.

Sword—Conquest is indicated.

Cup—You will be rewarded for a sacrifice you are about to make.

8

Dice and Dominoes

One of the oldest methods of fortune-telling is sortilege, or the casting of lots. In ancient China, coins were tossed into turtle shells to predict the future. Dice, not so different from those we know today, were originally made from the ankle bones of sheep and were used for divination by primitive people in distant ages and far-off lands—and also by some tribes of American Indians. Dominoes, which resemble two flattened dice laid side by side, were invented much later, in the eighteenth century. You can tell fortunes with either dice or dominoes. By the way, the gypsies say that dice and dominoes should never be read on a Monday or Friday. Also, it is considered extremely dangerous to read your own fortune by means of dice or dominoes on *any* day of the week.

If you are using dice, place two in a cup and throw them out, with some flare and ceremony, onto a piece of paper or cloth on which you have drawn a circle. Attempt to throw them inside the circle, but if one of them falls outside simply announce to the questioner that obstacles lie in the path to success. If both go out you may feel a bit clumsy, but the meaning is clear—a quarrel is about to take place. Take both dice and throw again, this time taking care to keep them within the circle.

If you are reading fortunes with dominoes, place all dominoes face down on a table. Have the questioner move them about to shuffle their order completely, and then have him pick one with his left hand. Read only this one domino.

The following list of meanings can be consulted either for a single domino or for the combination of dots on two dice:

6–blank:	Watch out! Scandal is threatened by this domino.
6–1:	You will marry twice and the second marriage will be the happier of the two.
6–2:	Good luck in business matters.
6–3:	Someone is going to give you a gift.
6–4:	Early marriage and many children are predicted.
6–5:	If you are looking for a job, you are about to find one. If not, this indicates a particularly pleasant day with a friend.
6–6:	Happiness lies ahead.
5–blank:	An unhappy marriage is predicted.
5–1:	A love affair or a proposal, or perhaps just an important social gathering.
5–2:	You will be defeated in an attempt to attain public office.
5–3:	A visitor is coming.
5–4:	A surprise, and soon. This will make you very happy.
5–5:	A fortunate change, which may be a new house.
4–blank:	For a farmer this means good crops. For others, money troubles.
4–1:	Troubles with debts are indicated. Also childless marriage.

4–2:   A loss by theft. Watch out.

4–3:   Happiness in love.

4–4:   You will have an invitation to a party.

3–blank: Trouble will come from too much love of money.

3–1:   A business trip is indicated and it should be successful.

3–2:   An old debt will be paid.

3–3:   A really large amount of money is coming your
way.

2–blank: This domino indicates poverty.

2–1:   An old friend is coming to visit.

2–2:   Your wish will be granted.

1–blank: An enemy is threatening your happiness.

1–1:   A reunion with someone you haven't seen in many
years.

Blank–blank: Unexpected trouble.

You may, after giving this reading, have the questioner draw
another domino, or you may throw the two dice again. This time
add up the dots and tell the client that, whereas the first reading
concerned happenings in the next month, this reading will foretell something that will occur during the coming year.

12 (6–6): You will meet someone in school or at a job who will
introduce you to a new and absorbing sport or hobby.

11 (6–5): You will part with a friend who may have been very
helpful to you in the past. The parting will come about
because one of you moves to another city.

10 (6–4 or 5–5): Your entire routine is about to be altered with
happy results. This will be caused by a change of school
or a change of job.

9 (6–3 or 5–4): Something very fortunate will happen during

the next year. It will be an important event and it is not something you expect at this time.

8 (6–2, 5–3, or 4–4): Watch out. Many troubles are coming and you are going to be the one to take the blame.

7 (6–1, 5–2, 4–3): A visitor is coming who will tell you something that will change your plans completely.

6 (6–0, 5–1, 4–2 or 3–3): You are about to lose money on an investment, or on a bet or in a game of chance. This can be avoided if you are on guard.

5 (5–0, 4–1, or 3–2): You are going to have problems at home. These may start with a clash with a sibling or a parent.

4 (4–0, 3–1, or 2–2): You are going to assume a position of leadership in your school, job, or community.

3 (3–0, 2–1): Something unexpected is going to happen. This is not going to bring happy results.

2 (1–1, 2–0): You will meet someone at a party who will affect your life.

1 (1–0): This is a symbol of misfortune.

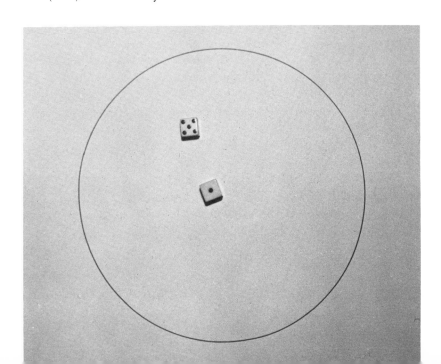

9
Crystal Ball Gazing

A lovely pink-tinged rock crystal ball, about as big as a large orange, is preserved today in the British Museum. It once belonged to John Dee, astrologer–fortune-teller to Queen Elizabeth I. You may not happen to have a crystal ball around the house, but if you do, try a bit of crystal ball gazing or scrying. Historically, scrying—the art of seeing images in glass balls or other clear surfaces—has been accomplished by looking into pools, wells, ink, blood, mirrors, sword blades, glasses of sherry. An offshoot of gazing into pools is the practice of wax reading, in which candle wax is dripped into cold water to congeal and form shapes which are then interpreted.

Scrying has been practiced throughout North and South America, Asia, Australia, and Africa, and is known virtually everywhere in the world in one form or another. Not everyone, of course, can accomplish this extremely mystical feat, which involves summoning up images or hallucinations by intense concentration. The old rules for crystal gazing state that you should first do some deep breathing to cleanse the blood and put you in proper shape for seeing things that aren't there. The ball should

Madam Freddie B. Jones, clairvoyant of Washington, D.C., looks into the future with the inspiration of her crystal ball.

be placed on a dark surface and the reader should sit with her back to the light (women are said to be more adept at scrying then men). When the image is about to appear the ball will become darker and darker and then—look deeply—look deeper . . . deeper . . . and concentrate.

If the ball becomes fingermarked or dusty, it should be cleaned by being boiled in a mixture of six parts water and one part brandy and then dried with chamois. No one but the questioner and the gazer should handle the ball. Reading should always be made when the moon is on the increase—in other words, expanding toward full moon.

Faces are often seen by crystal ball gazers. In rural towns in many countries, young girls walk three times around a well on certain saints' days and then look into the water to see the faces of the men they will marry.

Here are some of the other images you might see, particularly if you are clairvoyant.

White Clouds: Always a good sign.

Black Clouds: Always a bad sign.

The colors purple, green, or blue: This is a sign of joy, something marvelous will happen soon.

The colors red, orange, yellow: danger and trouble, sickness and loss, grief and betrayal.

Clouds moving upward: The answer to the question in the mind of the client is yes.

Clouds moving downward: The answer to the question in the mind of the client is no.

Shadows or clouds moving toward the gazer's right: This indicates that the spirits are interested in the well-being of the questioner.

Shadows or clouds moving toward the gazer's left: The ball-gazing session must be concluded immediately.

Having come to the end of this book you may consider yourself a qualified fortune-teller. From now on you will find that you are increasingly alert to bad signs and good vibrations. You will be sensitive to lucky numbers, wary of unlucky days, and considerably more understanding of your friends' strengths and weaknesses. You may even have gained some insights into your own personality and problems! Use your new skills imaginatively and responsibly. Remember that you are a beginner in the study of mysterious arts that others have practiced for a lifetime. There are still a great many secrets hidden in the stars, the cards, the tea leaves, and the crystal ball.

ANSWERS FOR ESP PICTURE TEST

1. Four
2. The one in her right hand
3. David (left)
4. Jane
5. Anne (above) and Alice (below)
6. Tony (center)
7 and 8.   In picture 7 it's Polly (right) and in picture 8 it's Margot (right)
9. Angela's
10. Green
11. a. Jonathan (front center)
    b. Josh (front left)
    c. Mika (back row, second from left)
12. His left hand

ACKNOWLEDGMENTS

Grateful acknowledgment is made to the following for the use of special material in this book:

The Curators of the Bodleian Library, Oxford, England, for the photographs on page 37. Reproduced by permission.

The Folger Shakespeare Library, Washington, D.C., for the photographs on pages 45 and 69. Reproduced by permission.

Mr. Ken Heinen, for the photograph on page 151.

Dr. Norman H. Horwitz, for the photographs on pages 26–29.

The Library of Congress, for the photographs on pages 112 and 114. Reproduced by permission.

The Pierpont Morgan Library, for the photographs on page 128, manuscript M. 630. Reproduced by permission.

Morgan Press, Inc., for permission to reproduce the tarot card designs from the Aquarian Tarot Deck on page 129 (left column).

Mr. Jonathan Morse, New York City, for permission to include the photograph on page 67 (right). Photograph courtesy of Fogg Museum, Cambridge, Massachusetts.

Mr. David Sinclair, for the drawings on pages 22 and 23 from *Mental Radio* by Upton Sinclair. Reproduced by permission.

The Smithsonian Institution, Freer Gallery of Art, Washington, D.C., for the photograph on page 67 (left). Reproduced by permission.

Tarot Productions, Inc., P.O. Box 46265, Los Angeles, Calif. 90046, for permission to reproduce the tarot card designs from the Albano-Waite deck on page 129 (right column).

U.S. Games Systems, for the tarot layout on page 132, and for the reproduction of the tarot card designs on page 129 (middle column). Used with permission.

The Author

Elinor Horwitz was born in New Haven, Connecticut, and lived there until her marriage to neurosurgeon Norman Horwitz, who is also the photographer of the ESP pictures in this book. Now living in Chevy Chase, Maryland, with their three children, the Horwitzes are avid collectors of books, Persian miniatures, and Islamic pottery. Professionally, Elinor Horwitz has written for many major national magazines and is a regular feature writer for the *Washington Evening Star*. In 1967 she attended the coronation of the Shah of Iran as a *Star* correspondent. Her first book, THE STRANGE STORY OF THE FROG WHO BECAME A PRINCE, was published in 1971.